Praise for *Ally Is a Verb*

"Reading Rose LeMay is like having tea with a really good friend. We know that really good friends not only support us, but also challenge us, and challenge leads to growth. LeMay asks all the right questions to take us beyond talk, advancing reconciliation as an action, a daily practice. As a citizen and as an ally, I am grateful to LeMay and for this book."
SHELAGH ROGERS, OC, Chancellor, Queen's University; Honorary Witness, Truth and Reconciliation Commission

"Rose LeMay offers all non-Indigenous Canadians an answer to their seemingly ever-present question 'What can I do?' when it comes to reconciling with Indigenous Peoples. This book is an all-in-one. It exposes the Great Canadian Lie; it teaches, educates, and offers concrete, pointed examples every settler can take to improve the future of everyone living in this country we call Canada. LeMay's book offers everyone a path forward on reconciliation. Everyone, go buy this book."
TANYA TALAGA, author, *All Our Relations* and *The Knowing*

"Every non-Indigenous person needs to read this transformative book. A history lesson, a coaching session, and a hopeful love letter to Canada, Rose LeMay's writing breaks down hard and difficult concepts in a way that is both accessible and achievable. After reading this book, each reader will be empowered to act."

JULIE CAFLEY, PHD, Executive Director, Catalyst Canada

"Truth before Reconciliation. Rose LeMay shares critical moments in Canadian history that laid the foundation for Canadian denialism of Indigenous peoples in this country and its hidden truths. I took pause. I took some deep breaths. I laughed, I hurt, I reflected, I empathized. I felt. This book is for all Canadians. Together, we can do more and you can say more. You too can be an ally on Team Reconciliation—start with step one and read this book."

KLUANE ADAMEK, Regional Chief, Assembly of First Nations, Yukon Region

"In this moment of intensified violence worldwide, joining Team Reconciliation can, as Rose LeMay teaches us, lead us along—and help us model for the world—a peaceful path toward better understanding, truth, justice, well-being, and reconciliation. We owe it to our Indigenous hosts, friends, and neighbours; we owe it to ourselves, our integrity, and our humanity; and we owe it to the world, to show we have the courage and strength to take this challenging hike in Canada, to face the discomfort and to step up for Indigenous communities. It's on us, and *Ally Is a Verb* makes plain the tools we need. LeMay gently guides us toward a common purpose and the mutual benefit that kinetic allyship can bring with a powerful theory of change, gentle pointers and resources, and unforgettable stories, inviting us along paths of continuous learning and practicing hope, so that together we can make real the promises of Canada. Thank you, Rose."

ANOUSH F. TERJANIAN, PHD, Fellow, Human Rights Research and Education Centre, University of Ottawa

"Rose LeMay emphasizes the importance of vulnerability, humility, and discomfort in being a true ally for Indigenous reconciliation, urging readers to ask questions and engage with Indigenous people to better understand their experiences. The steps and resources throughout the guide reflect LeMay's commitment to care, honesty, and the essential role of meaningful action in driving real change. She demonstrates how reconciliation requires allies who are knowledgeable, committed, and ready to take daily action, challenging the status quo and aligning with Canadian values of accountability and equality. Through a deep exploration of Indigenous Peoples' experiences that shaped the Truth and Reconciliation Commission's 94 Calls to Action, LeMay shows how modern Canada can become the inclusive and just country we aspire to be only when non-Indigenous people answer the call to confront historical injustices and take concrete steps toward real change."

BROOKE DELONG, founder, Connected Strategic Advisory Inc.

ALLY
IS
A VERB

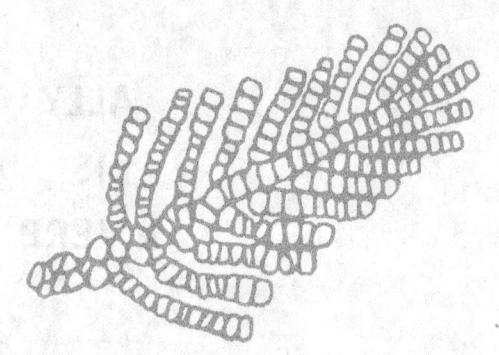

Rose LeMay

ALLY IS A VERB

A Guide to Reconciliation with Indigenous Peoples

PAGE TWO

Copyright © 2025 by Rose LeMay

All rights reserved. No part of this book may be reproduced, stored in a retrieval system or transmitted, in any form or by any means, without the prior written consent of the publisher or a licence from The Canadian Copyright Licensing Agency (Access Copyright). For a copyright licence, visit accesscopyright.ca or call toll free to 1-800-893-5777.

Cataloguing in publication information is available from Library and Archives Canada.
ISBN 978-1-77458-577-1 (paperback)
ISBN 978-1-77458-658-7 (ebook)

Page Two
pagetwo.com

Cover and interior design by Fiona Lee
Cover photo and beading by Heather Dickson
Interior illustrations by Lucie Raymond

Distributed in Canada by Raincoast Books
Distributed in the US and internationally by Macmillan

25 26 27 28 29   5 4 3 2 1

the-irg.ca

*For the next generation of Tlingit leaders,
may you stand tall so as to not be small.*

Allies need enough knowledge about Canada's history of racism against Indigenous people to recognize the long-term effects on all of us, enough capacity in their own culture and values to make room for people from other cultures, enough courage to see the current systems still holding back Indigenous people, and enough commitment to fix those systems. We do this work now, so we don't leave it for our children to do later. It's on us.

CONTENTS

Putting Allyship into Action *1*

1 **Reconciliation Starts with You** *7*

2 **Unpacking the Great Canadian Lie** *31*

3 **Challenging Interpersonal Racism** *65*

4 **Challenging Institutional Racism** *85*

5 **Lending Your Voice, Influence, and Privilege** *101*

6 **Getting Comfortable with Discomfort** *127*

7 **Finding Hope and Vision** *153*

Acknowledgements *169*

Notes *173*

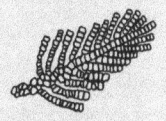

STATEMENT ABOUT THE TRADITIONAL MEDICINE COLLECTION COVER ART

"My grandmother's life work was learning and practicing with Traditional Medicines. I remember being a grumpy teenager getting dragged out of bed super-early to go harvest medicines with her on the weekends. When I reflect back to those memories and those teachings, they are some of my most favourite. Every flu season she'd have a big glass pot on the stove full of traditional teas, an Indigenous version of Buckley's and Cold-FX, if you will. She would give me a shot glass with some tea every morning and the years I lived with her I never got sick. I remember I was stung by a few wasps and she quickly grabbed some leaves, chewed them up and placed them on the stings and it soothed them. When I had cuts she'd place balsam sap on them and they would heal much faster. Her work with Traditional Medicines was magical and that's what I tried to capture in this collection, to turn these common northern plants into gorgeous wearable art pieces that reflect the powerful medicine they hold."

HEATHER DICKSON
from Carcross/Tagish First Nation, Dickson Designs

PUTTING ALLYSHIP INTO ACTION

On a beautiful day years ago on the west coast, I was teaching a group of adults about reconciliation. We talked about the importance of Indigenous cultures, the hidden history of Canada, current-day inequities in Indigenous health outcomes, and the strength and resilience of Indigenous people. A young white man was sitting at the back of the group and seemed to give me attitude all day. It wasn't over-the-top attitude, but it was enough that I kept my eye on him, as he didn't seem to be engaged. At the end of the day in the sharing circle, when it was his turn, he looked straight at me, and spoke loudly, "I'm angry, Rose!" It was a "facilitator moment," and I had to stay calm and simply listen as we were in a sharing circle.

But then the young man shared that his parents raised him on the prairies to hold racist views against

First Nations. And he clarified that he was so angry that he had missed out on being friends with First Nations people; he had missed out on knowing First Nations people his whole life, but it was going to change *now*. I gasped. And this young man changed my life. Thank you.

At that time in my career, I had a theory that non-Indigenous Canadians would care about reconciliation if they only knew about the history and racism, if they only knew about the problem that reconciliation would solve. I was attempting to apply change management approaches to reconciliation. Many told me it wasn't necessary as "Canadians should just go learn what they need to know." Except Canadians were not generally learning more about reconciliation, and we were not progressing as a country together, so what was holding us back? I started to build a change management approach into my teaching: here's the problem, here's the solution, do you want to be part of the solution? I believed that Canadians would care about Indigenous people if they knew more about our real history instead of the whitewashed version, started thinking of us as neighbours instead of as strangers. And this young man showed an adult's most dramatic possible response to learning: he learned more and immediately chose to be part of the solution.

As a facilitator in the field of anti-racism and reconciliation, I've seen more than my share of resistance from adults, from straight-up racism against Indigenous people all the way through to denial of Indigenous experience, which sounds like, "Can't you just get over it; it wasn't that bad." I've also witnessed moments of brilliance from learners as they grasped what they had not been taught in schools or by their families: Indigenous people are just truly amazing.

Becoming a next-level ally

The constant refrain I have heard in all my facilitation and public speaking is the question from allies "But what do I do?" This book is for non-Indigenous allies who already know they want to do something but are not sure about the next steps. Consider this a guide on how to be a next-level ally for reconciliation.

Allies start with enough literacy to do no harm. You need to know enough about Indigenous people to use the correct terms, enough about history to see the blatant acts done against Indigenous people in the name of Canada, and enough about current-day inequities Indigenous people face. *The more that you know, the more opportunity you will see to act as an ally.* Next-level allies use their skills to influence the people around them, especially those who disagree, to start their reconciliation journeys. The important work of an ally is to challenge racism against Indigenous people, and to challenge those who stand to benefit if we don't do reconciliation. Some people out there don't want reconciliation to succeed, and you likely have influence with them. Because the job of an ally is to change systems that aren't working for Indigenous people. Yes, there may be hard days, and you too can find comfort out on the land. Continue to build your skills, your practice to become a next-level ally. Continue to bring others along with you to join Team Reconciliation.

A few notes about terminology. I use the word "Indigenous," which describes all First Nations, Inuit, and Métis. I use the term "Indigenous people" to describe the various Indigenous individuals you meet in your daily life and workplace, and I use the term "Indigenous Peoples" to describe the three distinct groups in a legal sense of First Nations, Inuit, and Métis. I use the word "settler" to describe Canadians who are not Indigenous. I suggest we get comfortable with this word, rather than fight about semantics. There are settlers of European descent whose families have been here for generations, and settlers from all parts of the world who have come here in the last few years. Given that you picked this book up and have read this far, I'm going to assume you're okay with the word "settler," have even spent time thinking through how you have benefitted from the land that is traditional territory.

Allies are about action more than the words. Allies know that the 94 Calls to Action of the Truth and Reconciliation Commission (TRC) are more than the words; it is the heart and morality of them that matters. The

Calls to Action are intended to "redress the legacy of residential schools and advance the process of Canadian reconciliation." These were an outcome of the TRC's work to document the truth, from survivors and their families and communities, about the Indian residential school system in Canada. The commission's Final Report and Calls to Action were released in 2015.

To Indigenous readers, Elder Woody Morrison said that we are royalty with lineage going back countless generations. The knowledge that Indigenous cultures hold, given to us by the land and stars, predates all science, all healthcare, all education. Of the TRC's 94 Calls to Action, almost all of them are for settlers. Indigenous people are responsible for doing our part for only a few of those Calls to Action, and we are well underway. It's about the healing that we have already started, and it is about bringing back the pride in being Indigenous. We come from the stars. I also believe that some of the biggest changes in Canada have been supported by allies, and it would have taken us longer to achieve those goals without their support. So this book is for allies to step up and do the work of challenging racism, to change systems to eradicate the racism, and ultimately to believe—and act on the belief—that Indigenous Peoples belong and have immeasurable value to Canada.

I am Tlingit, Crow Clan of the Ishkìtan House. My mother comes from Taku River and my great-grandmother was Lucy Yàník Anderson. My father comes from Carcross, and my great-grandmother was Edith Mary Jackson. I am here because my ancestors survived residential schools. I am deeply honoured to have learned from Elder Woody Morrison, who was Haida and Tlingit, and Elder Mason Durie from Aotearoa. I am deeply honoured to learn from Knowledge Keepers who are Inuit; First Nations from Turtle Island and Australia, Hawai'i, and the United States; Métis; and Sámi. I apologize in advance to my teachers if I make errors in my speech and do my best to hold knowledge with respect.

1
RECONCILIATION STARTS WITH YOU

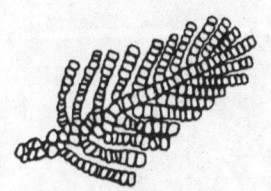

Where do you begin telling

someone their world is not the only one?

LEE MARACLE, *Stó:lō Nation*

WILLIAM CARPENTER BOMPAS was born in London, England, in 1834. He did not do well in his first profession of law, tried then quit the Baptist church, and was ordained in the Anglican Church in 1859. After a few stints in churches in England, the church sent him in 1865 to the "wild" of Rupert's Land, what is now northern Canada. After a post in Fort Simpson, he became the first bishop of the district of Athabasca in 1874. This district includes Tlingit land, our backyard, at a time when Tlingit communities were living their knowledge systems in relationship with and respect for the land.

Bompas, like most other men of England of his time, didn't see the beauty of the land or people; he only saw heathens in need of intervention. He tore our community and family apart in the name of a god from another place, and within a few years this whole wicked approach to "save us from ourselves" was funded by the infant Canadian government. He was the schools' architect in the North, there to save us from our savageness, us poor Indians. And he was a criminal.

Bompas died in 1905 and was buried in the Carcross Cemetery, surrounded by my Tlingit ancestors, like a rock in the middle of the flowers. Right beside his grave is the grave of a child, a Carcross Tlingit five-year-old who was likely one of the first children to die at Bompas's Carcross residential school, under his watch. A child of my ancestors who didn't make it.

It didn't have to be like this.

There are almost 700 First Nations, Inuit, and Métis communities in this country we call Canada, and every one of them has a similar story about people in robes coming to tell them they are uncivilized, unworthy. It wasn't just the churches. It was also the black suits of the federal government, sometimes alongside early provincial government men. And it wasn't just governments. It was other Canadian settlers who turned their eyes rather than care.

It didn't have to be like this.

Generations of Indigenous children were lost to the system of residential schools. Generations of Indigenous people were crushed almost to oblivion by colonization. We survived.

But it didn't have to be like this.

So now the country is doing reconciliation, because it did not have to be like this.

Some say "reconciliation" is an empty word because the dictionary meaning of it suggests a rebuilding of relationships between Indigenous people and settlers, but there was no such relationship to begin with. Some say reconciliation is irrelevant, because governments are not doing enough of it fast enough. Some see reconciliation as a conundrum, because it is a call for human rights in a country that prides itself on defending human rights yet doesn't do it at home. Some see reconciliation as a call to action as required by the TRC. Some see reconciliation as their personal responsibility to Indigenous neighbours.

Some people find it confusing to know who is supposed to do reconciliation and what it will look like when we're done. Here's the Coles Notes version: Reconciliation is up to non-Indigenous Canadians from coast to coast to coast to learn enough about the reasons why it is needed, to deepen their knowledge and capacity to see the current inequities facing Indigenous people, and then to do their part for reconciliation by fixing those inequities. We will know that we are getting close to being done when Indigenous people have similar health and well-being outcomes as any other group in Canada, and when Canada is proud to be an Indigenous country.

A lot of background context is needed for that last sentence to make sense. You would have to know the drastic differences in health outcomes for Indigenous people compared to non-Indigenous Canadians in life expectancy, chronic disease, and mental wellness. Another Coles Notes explanation: the differences in health outcomes between Indigenous people and non-Indigenous Canadians are like those between Sudan and Canada. Shouldn't we care about things like that? For a country that prides itself on human rights, this seems to be an oversight.

The context behind that sentence about being an Indigenous country is quite significant. Can you imagine the changes needed, the racism erased, the trust built, the relationships strengthened to get there?

Change and reconciliation

The TRC's Final Report, released in 2015, included 94 Calls to Action aimed at reconciliation following residential schools, but so little has been done to date. By 2023, only thirteen Calls to Action were considered complete by Yellowhead Institute, an Indigenous research centre associated with Toronto Metropolitan University. Many of those efforts were largely symbolic. One example is that after 2015, land acknowledgements became the norm but the lack of clean water in so many First Nations communities persisted, with no end in sight. Land acknowledgements without action are symbolic, and we demand more than symbolism. Perhaps reconciliation is irrelevant to most Canadians? More likely is that reconciliation has yet to make sense to most Canadians, because the history that Canada tells itself leaves out the whole story about Indigenous people.

But something did happen that changed everything.

On May 27, 2021, I sat waiting for the news release by Tk'emlúps te Secwépemc on the finding of over two hundred unmarked graves at the site of the Kamloops Indian Residential School in British Columbia. I had been forewarned of the news by a good friend, so I prepared myself to watch the event live. Having heard testimonies of survivors of residential schools from family members and others at events held by the TRC, I am familiar with the stories of children dying in these institutions. "Story," in this context, means truth. First Nations use the word "story" to mean testimony and knowledge. Indigenous children died from childhood diseases just like other children, but nobody cared to provide medical supports to Indigenous communities, so the death toll from tuberculosis in some schools, in some decades, was 50 percent or higher. I have also heard of the deaths of children through nefarious actions of school workers, which nobody dared to document as the abuse seemed unthinkable. There are really too many stories to ignore about the deaths of children in these institutions. Just to add to the pain, the police in the early 1900s did not even believe Indigenous people were humans with rights, so they never would have investigated any complaints. Knowing all this, I assumed I was prepared for the psychological and spiritual toll of the findings from Tk'emlúps te Secwépemc. The news still hit with all the weight of generations of loss.

But something was different this time. Over the next few days, non-Indigenous acquaintances—who had never spoken to me about Indigenous news—reached out to me to talk about residential schools. Many shared their deep sense of shame and remorse for not informing themselves about these institutions. Some called to apologize. Close allies called to make sure I was doing okay. It felt like something had finally shifted as non-Indigenous Canadians took responsibility for their roles in furthering reconciliation.

Following the news of the unmarked graves, I was shocked when Canadians from coast to coast to coast demanded not only that the Canadian flag fly at half-mast but that it continue for months, for the first time in the country's history. Canadians laid children's shoes on church steps and then publicly condemned anyone who removed them. Indigenous people were top of mind for Canadians for the first time.

As further discoveries of unmarked graves adjacent to residential schools continued, I felt like the country came to a guilty grinding halt. Canadians were finally learning the unvarnished version of their country's history.

Canadians were finally facing the truth that publicly funded residential schools were not in fact schools but prisons where children were forcibly placed and faced indoctrination, starvation, abuse, and death. It was a shift of titanic proportions.

The Great Canadian Lie

For a country that prides itself on defending human rights, Canada has held on to certain myths about its dealings with Indigenous people. For generations, Canada believed that there was good intent in its dealings with Indigenous people—didn't the federal government mean to do well with its attempts to help Indigenous people? The fact is there was no good intent toward Indigenous people. Governments and new settlers to this land believed Indigenous people were less-than, savage, uncivilized. The pervasive belief was that it was up to the white saviour to swoop in and save the Indians from themselves. New settlers and voters were convinced that Indians wanted this kind of help and did not know any better. Call it the Great Canadian Lie: "Canada gives with benevolence, and still the Indians don't get better. We're doing the best we can."

The Great Canadian Lie is one of the most sophisticated piles of racism ever. The so-called benevolence or charity was a cover-up used to extract as much land

and natural resources as possible, right out from under our feet. One of the most effective ways to break a community's will is to steal its children. Residential schools were all part of an attempt to remove Indigenous people from the land that the early settlers wanted.

After the Tk'emlúps te Secwépemc media release, there were still voices trying to make a case that unmarked graves represented the work of a "few bad apples" among the hundreds of teachers and priests who "meant well." Some claimed these unmarked graves must have been simply "accidents" on the part of the government and churches. I understand the resistance to this news that residential schools contributed to the deaths of children in this country, as Canada has a reputation for fairness and equity. But spelling out the truth is one way to uphold the memories and voices of the children who didn't make it. This is not the time to avoid the truths.

The truth always comes out, no matter how difficult it is to hear. Additional communities announced searches and findings of more and more unmarked graves. The unmarked graves revealed the structural racism that justified these schools and infected their teachers to allow for children to die. It opened the door to discussions of the ways that racism was implemented across history and used to justify the chronic underfunding of social supports for Indigenous people across Canada. Canadians started to talk about the generations-long funding inequities, the lack of compassion that churches, police, governments must have maintained for decades.

Many in leadership in this country were intentionally racist against Indigenous people, across decades upon decades. And there's proof, such as the legalization of racism in the Indian Act, the problematic law designed by the Canadian government as a tool of colonization. And the intentional underfunding of Indigenous health resources for generations. And the apartheid of "Indian hospitals," another form of institution just for Indigenous people that were also underfunded. When tuberculosis was increasing dramatically through residential schools and in Indigenous communities, the federal government set up separate Indian hospitals, but they were not really hospitals. Just as the schools were really not for education, these hospitals were not for receiving medical care—they were a way to segregate Indigenous people. They were known for non-consensual treatment (against the law then and now), medical experimentation, and abuse. Indian hospitals were not generally known as healing places. This is the history that allies need to know; otherwise it is too easy to buy into the "bad apples" myth.

Just accidents? Bad apples? Buckets and bushels of bad apples.

The strongest myth of all in this country also died on May 27, 2021—the myth of benevolence, the Great Canadian Lie. The voices of the children were finally heard, and I believe the era of reconciliation has finally started.

Reconciliation in a global context

Canada is not the first country to commit to a process of reconciliation. Canada joins a list of countries, including South Africa and Germany along with others, who have consciously made policy to diminish the rights and well-being of a minority and/or enacted war against a minority population.

South Africa is known for its apartheid against Black citizens, and perhaps less so for its decades-long work on reconciliation. Nelson Mandela is best known for his work bringing together Black and settler South Africans. South Africa chose to do reconciliation in the courtroom but without expectation of retribution for perpetrators. Witnesses gave testimony in the sanctuary of the courts, and judges oversaw the process. There is one significant difference between South Africa's reconciliation for apartheid and Canada's reconciliation for residential schools, and it is that Canada chose to do reconciliation based in relationship and healing, as opposed to in the courts. Canada chose the commission route, hence the TRC.

The Treaties signed with many (but not all) First Nations stressed partnership and relationship between Indigenous people and settlers, a sign of the fundamental values of First Nations. These values were carried into negotiations about how the country would embark on reconciliation with Indigenous people, with a mention that survivors would probably feel safer sharing their stories in circle with mental health supports instead of in a courtroom. There also may have been a sense by the federal government that it might be in its best interest to never step into a courtroom to explain its crimes. In the end, Canada chose a relational and healing approach to reconciliation. It's an important distinction, as South African courts probably had more force than Canada's commission. We relied on the people doing the right thing out of relationship and morality, rather than through legal enforcement. We continue to rely on Canadians in positions of leadership to enact reconciliation out of good will, rather than force it upon people by law.

Rwanda fell into civil war in the early 1990s and over 800,000 Tutsi were killed as well as thousands of Hutu. In this brutal season, neighbours turned on each other. The country's reconciliation process took a traditional dispute resolution approach, where survivors shared their stories while perpetrators listened. If they chose, perpetrators were also given space to apologize. Rwanda did not do a court process looking for facts and criminal charges, and the country is held up as a model in the world. Canada's approach was similar, with survivors sharing their experiences, but the churches/perpetrators attended only in the form of representatives of organizations there to witness the proceedings, not to take accountability. And somehow the Canadian federal government did not participate as a perpetrator but kept its distance; it had a decision-making and oversight role, participating as an observer rather than a guilty actor.

Germany went through a process of reconciliation following the Holocaust—the genocide of Jewish people and others. Leaders of war crimes were charged by the newly constructed International Court of Justice, and billions of dollars were assigned in war debt. The country endured some of the largest monetary fines ever imposed for crimes against humanity and only paid them off in 2010.

There are valuable lessons from Germany. Following World War II and the international condemnation and penalties applied to the country for murders of civilians and genocide, a domestic period of silence, during which nobody talked about the Holocaust, lasted years. Almost every German family had a family member who fought for the Nazis, and that's difficult to fathom given the human tendency to declare that evil is what *others* do. So Germany practiced benevolence and the bad-apple denial system just like Canada has: "It wasn't all of us; it was just a few of them who did it." Flash forward through a quiet forty years and the German government made a significant policy decision to teach about the Holocaust in schools including field trips to Holocaust Memorial sites. It turns out that education is the equalizer to overcome denial of history. There are so many lessons from Germany's road of redemption, and here is only one: Humans have a remarkable tendency to deny history if it involves guilt or pain, but history must be taught well in schools if we want to have a hope of democracy.

Which brings this story back to Canada. Canada started its reconciliation journey just a handful of years after the last residential school was shut down in the 1990s, much faster than any other country has attempted. We are still in the era of truth and learning about the wrongs done to Indigenous people in the name of Canada, while we are also attempting to do reconciliation. So it probably feels awkward to be talking about the moral duty of it while some Canadians still doubt that children even died at the residential schools. It might have been easier to spend a few years building on the truth side before starting reconciliation, and some provinces and territories are teaching about the past, but probably not about the present inequities facing Indigenous people. But we really don't have the time to spend ten or twenty years educating to fill in knowledge gaps; we do not have the time to drag it out now. Every delay in doing the work of reconciliation is essentially reinforcing systems that risk Indigenous lives. You need to know enough about the current-day racism and inequities that Indigenous people face, as this is what creates the urgency to change things. We don't have time to slow-walk reconciliation.

Reconciliation is
a societal change, and societal
changes are brought about
by regular people influencing
others around them.

Canada chose to do a relational approach to reconciliation rather than a legal approach, so education is even more important because there is no law to enforce it.

We can't wait for governments to lead

And herein lies the significant barrier to reconciliation progress. Reconciliation relies on individuals to do the right thing, corporate leaders to do the right thing in companies, and Canadians to do the right thing for reconciliation. No law requires companies to hire Indigenous people and so contribute to closing the gap for Indigenous employment. No law requires politicians to represent Indigenous people in their riding, nor for media to cover events involving Indigenous people. No law with measurable outcomes requires the federal government to act on the TRC Calls to Action, nor for any government to fulfill them. Things are vague. There is no consequence in the law for slow-walking reconciliation or for governments dodging the responsibility for real change to ensure Indigenous people's well-being.

But herein also lies the secret power of Canadians from coast to coast to coast. Canadians don't need governments to tell them to do the right thing for Indigenous neighbours. Canadians are the leaders in reconciliation. Individuals influence their book clubs to read Indigenous authors, take their families to pow wows to learn from Indigenous neighbours, watch Indigenous-directed movies, and walk alongside Indigenous people to demonstrate for Indigenous human rights. CEOs of big companies lead their employees to partner with Indigenous people, boards of non-profits commit to include Indigenous board members, and organizations honour the National Day for Truth and Reconciliation as a staff learning day.

Reconciliation in Canada is being led in neighbourhoods, corporations, and organizations. You practice the skills with friends and family, and then you take it to work. It is a good thing, because if you want to change the world, the fastest way to do it is with the people you know in your personal and professional networks. If every single company and organization and service commits to being a safe place for Indigenous employees and clients, that will indeed change the world for Indigenous employees and clients.

Citizens are miles ahead of governments on reconciliation. But the country still has work to do, and this book is for the allies who want to lead that work in their communities and networks.

Reconciliation is a societal change, and societal changes are brought about by regular people, in neighbourhoods and in workplaces, influencing others around them. That movement for reconciliation builds and ripples across a whole sector, and then into neighbouring sectors and cities through some healthy peer pressure. Next thing you know, society is changing.

This is my theory of reconciliation: Reconciliation relies on individuals choosing to learn more about Canada's history of genocide and working through the pain that new knowledge can sometimes bring. But reconciliation doesn't stop there. It must continue; just like athletes practice and deepen skills for their sport, allies must also deepen knowledge and skills to make change. You continue to learn more about the current inequities endured by Indigenous people, because the more knowledge you have, the more opportunity you will see to take your place in fixing those inequities—including how to see and challenge racism against Indigenous people. You learn and practice how to be a change agent. Reconciliation relies on you learning more to do better. The more we build up an army of allies for reconciliation, the more pressure we can put on governments of all stripes to fulfill their responsibilities for reconciliation. We need allies with the knowledge, commitment, and capacity to practice their influence daily and join the team to make real change in this country.

I am often accused of trying to change the world, as if this is a bad thing. What if the world that is in your influence (your family, community, and workplace) is the focus of reconciliation? Then we indeed can change the world. The truth is that the next Indigenous individual who walks through your world, and is fully accepted and respected, that this might change that Indigenous individual's world. You can do the work to create belonging in your world for Indigenous people. You can lead change in community and in workplaces.

Reconciliation is local.

A note about discomfort

I suspect my tone up to now might have raised a few eyebrows. Provocative, perhaps. The truth is that I'm using my toned-down educator voice, as I need you as an adult learner to continue in your learning journey. Rest assured that I do have strong emotions about how my ancestors were treated and how Indigenous people continue to be mistreated in healthcare and by police at alarming rates. In this context, I speak as an adult educator. I need to you to be able to hear me.

Adult education teaches that adults need to feel safe enough to learn. We don't do well learning while under fire. But here is an ironic twist: For adults to learn, we also have to be just a bit uncomfortable, just like how an athlete pushes muscles to develop through exercises and experiences a bit of pain. When we feel comfortable, we are likely faced with information that we already know, reinforcing what we know. And that feels good; it's comfortable. Conversely, being presented with new information takes work. You have to think it through, compare it to the files inside your brain, and perhaps even refile some of it or start new files. It's work. It's uncomfortable.

Learning more and adding new information about the history of Canada's impacts on Indigenous people is uncomfortable because of the content. So it may be new information, and it may also be distressing information that hits some emotional buttons.

And there's a third aspect to this discomfort. Being an ally is essentially about practicing new skills in the real world with Indigenous people; there is no sandbox to try it out in, far away from witnesses. There will be discomfort.

But discomfort is not fatal. It is a sign that you are learning, trying new skills, and expanding yourself as a human. It's a sign of growth. Lean into discomfort. Welcome to Team Reconciliation and the next stage of your growth as an ally.

NEXT STEPS

Read three to four testimonies of survivors in *The Survivors Speak: A Report of the Truth and Reconciliation Commission of Canada* (available at nctr.ca/records/reports/) or watch videos of survivors sharing their experiences on the Legacy of Hope Foundation website (legacyofhope.ca/wherearethechildren/stories/).

Learn more about the healing that survivors have chosen to do through the Canadian Geographic "Indigenous Peoples Atlas of Canada" (indigenouspeoplesatlasofcanada.ca/article/redress-and-healing/).

Take a few notes. What do you need to learn more about to fill in any gaps in your knowledge about Canada's history?

Pick at least three of the following ally actions to complete in the next month, and then pick another three to do in the following few months.

- Buy gifts from Indigenous artists and ask about the objects' meanings so you can spark a conversation with the recipient.

- Attend local Indigenous events such as a pow wow or gala. Give at fundraisers.

- Buy books by Indigenous authors, watch movies by Indigenous directors, and listen to podcasts by Indigenous producers.

- Do your research so you can answer the question "Where are you from?" using Native Land Digital (native-land.ca).

- Ask other allies what they are doing and share ideas.

- Bring Indigenous-authored books into your book club.

- Ask your elected leaders (municipal, provincial/territorial, and federal) about what they are doing for reconciliation.

- If you have children, talk to them about reconciliation, get them books by Indigenous authors, and check that their teachers are covering history appropriately.

- Volunteer at your local Indigenous health centre, friendship centre, or Aboriginal Head Start centre.

—— RESOURCES ——

Indigenous Reconciliation Group (IRG). *Indigenous Cultural Competence and Humility*. Online course. the-irg.ca/onlinecourses/.

National Inquiry into Missing and Murdered Indigenous Women and Girls. *Reclaiming Power and Place: The Final Report of* the National Inquiry into Missing and Murdered Indigenous Women and Girls.* Privy Council, 2019. mmiwg-ffada.ca/final-report/.

Truth and Reconciliation Commission of Canada. *Truth and Reconciliation Commission of Canada: Calls to Action.* 2015. the-irg.ca/docs/truth-and-reconciliation-commissions-calls-to-action/.

United Nations. *United Nations Declaration on the Rights of Indigenous Peoples.* 2007. the-irg.ca/docs/united-nations-declaration-on-the-rights-of-indigenous-peoples.

2

UNPACKING THE GREAT CANADIAN LIE

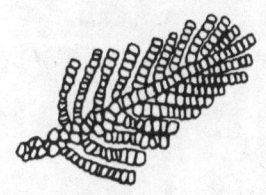

The circumstances of Indian existence prevents him following that course of evolution which has produced from the barbarian of the past the civilized man of today… He has been called upon suddenly and without warning to enter upon a new existence. Without the assistance of the Government, he must have failed and perished miserably and he would have died hard entailing expense and disgrace upon the Country.

J.A. MACRAE

IS THE QUOTE that opens this chapter a bit startling? J.A. Macrae, the Indian Affairs Department Inspector of the North West, in his time, met with no raised eyebrows. The quote is from 1886, and Macrae was actually on the moderate side compared to others who argued that the "Indians" would just die off and the only option for federal lawmakers was to stand by and watch. Canadian political leaders and nation builders in the past have said some nasty things and then turned around and told citizens that their action to keep Indigenous people down, or blatant inaction in the face of need, was the kind thing to do.

Perhaps reconciliation in Canada is moving slowly because the reason why we have to do it has not been fully shared and understood. A change management approach is to name the problem and the solution, and then to get people's buy-in to be part of the solution.

So here is the problem statement: Canada did unreasonably cruel things to Indigenous people across the history of this country to get at their land. It outlawed their cultures, restricted their movement, stole their children and lied about it, and refused to take accountability. And Canada continues to fight in court against giving Indigenous people equitable supports for healthcare and education, to the point of being forced to pay out billions in court-ordered settlements. Canadians might believe that Great Canadian Lie that Indigenous people just can't succeed on their own two feet and need the federal government to support them and, even worse, might personally act on racist beliefs that Indigenous people are not like others.

The solution is reconciliation, and it is multifaceted and somewhat complex: address history gaps for Canadians, stop racism, fix those inequitable systems so that Indigenous people have the supports that other Canadians have, and make sure we don't ever do genocide again.

That's a complex problem statement that reflects the criminality of Canada's past against Indigenous people, and then the additional challenge of the hidden motives tied up in racism. The solution statement has to address the systems that allowed the crimes against Indigenous people as well as the racism.

Except schools have not taught accurate Canadian history, and if adults do not have a good grasp of what really occurred, talking about the solution of reconciliation is difficult because the problem isn't clear. We have not come to grips fully with the crimes that Canada did to Indigenous people in the name of settlers. Canada is still holding on dearly to the myth that the early country builders did the best they could to help those Indigenous people out of their "savageness."

Reconciliation means first ditching the Great Canadian Lie. To do that, a short tour of history is required.

History is an interesting thing. The more we know, the more we can fill in the gaps in our knowledge. You may know some history and feel pride in being Canadian. Canada has an enviable international reputation for human rights and has supported the fight in many countries around the world. Canada's public health system is held up as an international model. Then there is our stable democracy, lacrosse, and hockey. All of that is true, yet there is still room to add more knowledge.

What follows is not an authoritative or a comprehensive tour of history. That has already been covered in the Royal Commission on Aboriginal Peoples, research by the TRC, and Tanya Talaga's book *The Knowing*. The short tour of history here is meant to paint a picture that shows why reconciliation is uniquely difficult in Canada.

A note to new Canadians who have recently moved here. Perhaps you escaped from a dangerous home and chose Canada because of its safety. That remains true—Canada is a safe country for most. In your research to become a Canadian, you likely did not hear about what Canada did to Indigenous people. This information may be startling, and yet, you are also asked to take your place as an ally for Indigenous people. The work for reconciliation, equity, and safety for Indigenous people will have positive impacts for everybody. When one of us is at risk, we are all at risk.

The stability before contact

Indigenous Peoples have a long history in what is now known as Canada. Thousands of years of complex governments, Treaties among ourselves, trade and economy, all the markers of civilizations existed here on Turtle Island long before anybody fell upon our shores. The Great Canadian Lie erased Indigenous Peoples and their ways of life to make way for a colonial white mark on the map. It's ironic that the lost people such as Jacques Cartier, the ones who were lost and stumbled onto our lands in the east, referred to themselves as the "civilized ones." University textbooks might note the Renaissance as the start of modern civilization and representative government in Europe, but in all honesty, Europe was pretty late to the game.

In Europe, the crusades between the Christians and Muslims went on from around 1095 until about 1300, a time when new town governments got their start and universities began to be built. Key building blocks of civilization were being established, while the religions conducted their bloody wars. Historians usually note the fourteenth century as the start of the Renaissance in Europe.

On Turtle Island, in the twelfth century, Takanawita brought the Iroquois Confederacy together with the Gayanashagowa, or Great Law of Peace, ending years of conflict between the five nations of the Haudenosaunee, in the area now known as Ontario, Quebec, and New York State. The Tree of Peace and its representational governance model is said to have influenced how the country of Canada was made, also with representation. The Great Law of Peace was highly successful as there has not been conflict within the five nations since.

The twelfth century marked yet another century of successful civilizations, with justice systems, education, and community governance for First Nations and Inuit across Turtle Island. Another century in a long history of thousands of years of local governance involving Treaties with neighbours for mutual support. Another century of complex civilizations. Indigenous Peoples had civilizations for thousands of years before the Renaissance in Europe. Do not believe part of the Great Canadian Lie that outsiders brought civilization to the savages here on Turtle Island—not even close.

What happened over a period of just a few hundred years to change the trajectory for Indigenous Peoples from stability to almost extinction? White supremacy. But the relationship between Indigenous people and white people who fell upon our shores did not start like that.

When the lost people landed on the shores of what we now call Canada in the 1400s, reportedly starting in the late 1490s, they would not have survived without the support of First Nations. First Nations on the east coast and new white settlers made numerous friendship agreements. But soon enough, more and more settlers came—to make a living, some to escape life in England and France at the time. Picture the time of Shakespeare in London, the prince in the castle and the pauper in the streets. And Marie Antoinette, the queen of France in the eighteenth century who is infamous for saying the phrase "let them eat cake" in response to being informed that bread was too expensive for poor people to buy. Cue the French Revolution. Or Charles Dickens's portrayal of nineteenth-century England in *A Tale of Two Cities*. All to say, these centuries were not a great time in England or France unless you were royalty or very rich. So some people came over here to find better lives. Then more and more people came over for the furs, timber, and a chance to get rich quick.

Beaver fur—who would have thought this would be high fashion? Remember the top hat? It was made from the felt or inner fur of a beaver. At the time of the fur trade and the expansion of settlers across what we now call Canada, the beaver-felt top hat was selling in

London for the equivalent of a small car today. It was seen as the height of fashion, a sign that you had made it. And it drove the fur trade and what is referred to as "exploration" from the 1600s to the 1800s across what is now known as Canada. The phrase "mad as a hatter" also came from the fur trade. Beaver felt was prepared using mercury nitrate, a poison that can cause all sorts of issues with the brain, including emotional instability and hallucinations. Hatters making the felt might have been exposed, hence the phrase "mad as a hatter."

In 1763, as more and more newcomers came over, the King of England wrote a decree to these explorers, these adventurers, saying, and I paraphrase, "Hey, don't take the land if there are people there already. You need to buy it if you want it." The decree is called the Royal Proclamation. Unfortunately, explorers did not like this declaration. They decided to interpret this Royal Proclamation as if the king were saying, "Don't take the land if there are 'civilized' people there, you know, real people. But if they are just savages...?" Explorers looked at the land and looked at the people who were already there, First Nations and Inuit, and said, "Wow, they don't dress like us, they don't build stone castles like us, they don't farm like us, they don't speak our language. They can't be civilized. Therefore, I can take the land. I'm going to put my peg in this empty land. It's mine."

As more explorers and settlers came to the east coast and into what is now known as central Canada, they started to outnumber Indigenous people. The old friendship agreements of the late 1400s and 1500s started to fall away. They were all broken by the 1700s and 1800s because settlers, in essence, did not want or need the partnership of First Nations anymore.

Unfortunately, the new settlers also brought diseases that had serious consequences for First Nations and Inuit. Flus, colds, smallpox, and tuberculosis all had serious impacts on Indigenous communities that had no resistance to these diseases. There was probably a local or regional epidemic in what we now call Canada every thirty to forty years across these centuries, including the Spanish flu in 1918–19. Having lived through the COVID pandemic, the historic pandemics now have a starkly different impact than simply a chapter in a book. Now we have a better understanding of what it would be like to live through an epidemic and to lose family members to disease. When smallpox hit First Nations communities on the west coast, up to 80 percent of people in some communities died. This story gets worse, because the new settler towns were built with racism and rarely, if ever, did settlers help First Nations communities during the crisis. For example, when a smallpox epidemic hit in 1862–63 in what is now British Columbia, colonial leaders in Victoria dithered and discussed how to help these communities, but in the end did not lift a hand to support their First Nations neighbours. Public health measures and support were not extended to First Nations.

Another story to portray the benevolence of the Great Canadian Lie, which really is malevolence, is about blankets. During the War of 1812, Americans started to pressure the British forces, and First Nations along the Canadian-American border decided to throw their support behind the British partly due to the fact that the American military was known for massacring Indigenous people in the Indian wars. As a result of the added military strength provided by First Nations, Canada won the War of 1812. But the British military did not like that First Nations had built up so much political power. An Elder from one of the communities shared a story of an event that happened a few years after the War of 1812, about the British military giving smallpox-infected blankets to the First Nation as a way to destroy their political weight. That is not charity. That is criminal.

The blankets might have been some Hudson's Bay point blankets with the stripes and the obscure slashes on one end. A slash or point on the blanket referred to the number of furs needed to trade for it. The more points, the heavier the blanket. All I can think about when I see these blankets is the way they were used in germ warfare against First Nations.

Policy chaos

During the rest of the 1800s, white men who were mostly British debated what to do with the "Indian problem" and produced many reports and papers, none of which referenced the input of Indigenous people themselves.

As an aside, please try to avoid the phase "Indigenous issue." I am not an issue, nor were First Nations in the 1800s "a problem."

Here is an example of the policy chaos at play. In the 1830s in Upper Canada, now part of Ontario, the men in suits debated four options to deal with the "Indian problem": extermination, slavery, insulation, or amalgamation. The extermination and slavery options are quite self-explanatory. A growing humanitarian movement in England thankfully advocated against these two options for the Indians. So insulation and amalgamation were on the table. Insulate First Nations away from civilization, because they would never be civilized. Or amalgamate (integrate) them through education to be civilized.

The Lieutenant-Governor of Upper Canada at the time, Sir Francis Bond Head, took the position that Indians were a doomed race and they would never be able to survive in a civilized world. He argued that Indians, especially those wandering Indians who did not have real houses, should be moved someplace where they could all die quietly on their own. He advocated that

Manitoulin Island be that place. White men debated the fate of Indians for years, but an influential factor was that England did not want to pay a single dollar more for those Indians. It was the start of frugality as a primary driver, instead of humanity.

Another important factor in the policy chaos, as the white men in suits saw it, was the complete lack of civilization of Indians. For example, the Indians' refusal to live in real houses in one place, or to believe in materialism and property like cows and ploughs. This led white men to believe that Indians would simply die off, as they couldn't "evolve" or act like civilized humans. So the federal government often simply did nothing in the face of need of Indigenous people, likely hoping the problem would just go away.

But then the humanitarian movement in England started, and Londoners who believed in humane policy started to lobby the Canadian government. Through their loud lobbying, even from London, outside influencers forced federal political leaders to do something. For the next 150 years, a mix of conflicting policy was enacted: Some support was given like a bandage to stop the bleeding but not to fix the underlying issues, versus some forceful policies requiring Indians to live like white people, and let's not leave out the times that the federal government did nothing.

For example, at one point in history the grand white men deemed that Indians must farm to be civilized and forced some communities to start farming. Then

Indigenous communities got so effective at it that they made more money than settler farmers. So the white powers told Indians to continue to farm but without any machinery. Do just enough to stave off the humanitarians back home in England, but don't let the Indians thrive. What a mess.

The early days of infant Canada

Now, imagine this: It's 1876, nine years after Canada became a country in 1867. Horse-drawn carts line the new settler-town streets, men are wearing top hats and long coattails, and women are wearing long dresses and petticoats. White traders and "adventurers" are pushing into First Nations lands to try to buy the land for cheap or simply cheat them out of it. Sitting Bull led his people into Canada to escape the US military war against them at the Battle of the Little Bighorn, and Alexander Graham Bell invented the telephone.

The late 1800s were also a time of blatant racism and patriarchy. English newspapers printed editorial cartoons about the weight of being white and having to care for all the savages. One drawing is of a white knight in glowing white armour riding a white horse, and the grateful savages kneel before him. The English writer Rudyard Kipling wrote about "the white man's burden" (with a poem by that name published in 1899), describing the perceived moral requirement of white men to save the non-white savages and barbarians and make them civilized.

In the world of politics, Canada's infant federal parliament was debating trade and protectionism versus free trade between its seven provinces and the grand North West Territories, which stretched from the borders of Ontario to British Columbia and into the Arctic, with Manitoba a postage stamp in the territory, at the bottom right of the map.

Parliament does not read like a play, so the debates were pretty bland stuff.

On Tuesday, March 21, 1876, federal parliamentarians discussed the draft bill regarding Indians. Parliament wanted to speed up the integration of Indians living like settlers in towns and to decrease the number of Indians living like in the "old days," although only those deemed to have "intellect" were eligible to apply for enfranchisement. A debate ensued about a provision that Indians who left their reserve would be at some point automatically "enfranchised," the word used to determine that an Indian was fully integrated into civilization and so no longer an Indian. The debate heard from those who wanted enfranchisement to happen quickly—to reduce the number of "Indians," as if they were problems to be erased. Others argued that it was not in Canada's best interest for Indians to interact with white people to learn their ways, and Indians shouldn't be punished for that. Back in the day, it was quite the courageous white man who advocated on behalf of Indians, but the advocates did not have enough impact. Of course, Indigenous people could not be elected officials and were not allowed in parliament, so the white men made the decisions.

The Honourable Mr. Langevin (Conservative), from Trois-Rivières, Quebec, rose to speak with all the knowledge he had. "Indians were not in the same position as white men. As a rule they had no education, and they were like children to a very great extent. They, therefore, required a great deal more protection than white men... Some general plan would have to be adopted to educate Indians and fit them for enfranchisement, just as a white boy would be prepared for manhood." This is the argument for fiduciary legal authority, that the new government would hold legal authority for Indians as if they were children, because they could not possibly make decisions like adults or care for themselves.

Must have been nice to be a parliamentarian in those days, having the power of gods themselves, debating the place and rights of another people who predated their families on this land. In hindsight, this debate about what do about the Indian problem is more ominous and inhumane than the Indian Act.

Canada's political leaders thought Indigenous people did not have the intellect to be civilized, but a sense of white supremacy led parliament to do "what was needed" to try to educate Indigenous people out of their

"Indian-ness," to protect those Indians from themselves. The Indian Act reflected Langevin's thoughts on the matter and enshrined that sense of fiduciary duty and gave the new federal government the decision-making power over Indians—as though they were children.

But there's another crucial layer to this. All the talk about fiduciary duty and the inability of Indians to make decisions and then the resulting Indian Act, this is all the foundation of the Great Canadian Lie—because the rhetoric and the legal doctrine were instruments for getting the land and natural resources away from the Indians. What better way than to call them children and simply take away their human rights and autonomy? Then they can't argue in any court against the theft. The Indian Act cemented in decades of similar actions to diminish the rights of Indigenous people, to limit their ability to stop progress, even to "get rid of the Indian problem." Duncan Campbell Scott led the federal Department of Indian Affairs in the 1920s, and he used that phrase to describe the intention of the Indian Act and the residential schools. Get rid of the problem (the people), and grab the land. And it's so much cheaper than having to buy it!

Don't make the mistake of believing this was benevolence or charity. This was the biggest steal in Canada's history. Millions of acres stolen in the façade of charity. And then the political leaders doubled down on Indians by withholding the supports given to other citizens and driving them into poverty. Then turned around in their long-tailed coats and told Canadians that those Indians want it this way. This is second half of the Great Canadian Lie.

The original Indian Act would be shockingly illegal if it were drafted as a bill today. Imagine trying to legalize theft and take away human rights using a racist rationale against a group of people today. This is the Canadian version of colonization. It was not a military takeover, it was racism at its worst through the façade of charity. Perhaps a military conflict would have been easier to heal from compared to this malevolent and effective approach to destroy a people. If you were the leader of an Indigenous community and saw an army storming over the hill, you would know who the enemy was. But Canada walked in smiling and held its hand out to shake, while the other hand was stealing our children and our land.

Keep in mind that even in 1876, as it is now, politicians made these decisions in the name of the Canadian public—the voters. They did it for settlers and companies to get access to resources without paying for them. Settler families who have been here for generations have benefitted from that Great Canadian Lie, from free land given to settler farmers, from inheritances from ancestors who made their money through those natural resources. Canada wouldn't exist without the theft of Indigenous land and removal of Indigenous people's rights.

I often wonder what my ancestors would have thought and felt as outsiders tried to erase them off the earth, tried to "civilize the Indian" out of them. What did my aunties and uncles think when they were unable to spend time with Elders in community and instead were forced to go to residential schools? What did my grandparents feel when they saw the threat of colonization enacted through laws of segregation and racism? How did they survive against all odds?

The past led to the present

Should we judge the old white men by the values that we hold today? If you're looking for a rationale to avoid judgement of past nation builders, fair warning that you will not find it here. The views of Bond Head, who said Indians should be left to die alone on Manitoulin Island, were harsh even by the values of the 1830s. I'm sure he did some nice things, but nice things do not matter when one advocates for the extermination of a people. But this review is not about judgement of the past decision-makers. This is about looking at the past to figure out where we are now.

The past in this country that we call Canada is completely papered over with white supremacy. What else can you call it when white men decide in closed rooms what to do about Indigenous people? What else can you call it when decisions that are based in racist beliefs of a group's inferiority are made about that group?

In 1876 the Indian Act was passed into law. On the surface it set out that the federal government alone would deal with First Nations, and do so community by community. The act targeted Indians and created segregation, discrimination, and reserves—lands set aside for Indians. Taku River Tlingit First Nation used to care for thousands of square kilometres stretching across Alaska, British Columbia, and the Yukon, in collaboration with neighbouring First Nations, and moved about for hunting and gathering to ensure that no one area would get hunted out. Our reserves are scattered about and total about five square kilometres now. Some First Nations negotiated through Treaties for their reserves, but many had no opportunity to do so.

The new federal government deemed it their role to deal with the Indian problem, and the brand-new provinces probably had enough on their plates anyhow. As governments love lists, they needed a list of who the Indians were, the real ones, so they developed a race-based membership list based on blood quantum. If you were at least 25 percent Indian blood then you got on the list, and the people on this status list—and nobody else—were eligible for the services from the new Department of Indian Affairs. But then the government changed the qualifications for how to get on this list, and then changed them again. All the changes resulted in a reduction in the number of Indians, never an adjustment to increase services to more people. The changes were to reduce the number of Indians, to reduce the cost to the new federal Department of Indian Affairs. Was it intentional? Absolutely. Frugality has always been the heart of Indian Affairs.

Inuit and Métis were not impacted by the Indian Act, and it's unclear whether the brand-spanking-new federal government in the 1870s even knew about Inuit. The Métis were treated differently; they were not met as communities but as individuals through scrip—a Métis head of the family could claim a portion of land instead of a community-based approach. Whether or not that was a better approach is hard to say, but it certainly battered the sense of the Métis as a community and nation.

Residential schools

And then there are the residential schools. Much has been written about them, so what I offer here is barely a snapshot of the loss and trauma that Indigenous people endured. The institutions that were set up to educate Indians were not about education. The white leaders of the day acted on their racist beliefs that Indians would never achieve the intellect of adults. These white leaders would never have built schools. They built institutions to train labourers for the white settler class. Churches were willing partners in this genocide, if only to save all those lost savages, and perhaps for the money from the new federal government to run the institutions.

Indigenous people have always valued education and wanted to ensure their children and youth understand their roles in communities. But every time in history when one group of people forces another group of people to use their customs, beliefs, and values, we call it colonization. And that's a bad thing. When it's done by force and thousands of children die, it's genocide.

The point of residential schools was to eliminate the Indian problem, to turn Indians into good labourers and servants who knew their lowly place in Canadian society. The first prime minister of Canada, John A. Macdonald, was one of those people who acted on white supremacist beliefs. He may hold a title of nation builder because he was around when maps were drawn, but he enacted racism as law in this country. He was one of the handful of white men who built the residential school policy and system. He essentially wanted Indians to know their place or die. The Indian Act set up Indian agents, employees of the Department of Indian Affairs, one stationed on each reserve. The agent had the power of government service delivery (or explicitly to deny services), police, justice, and healthcare all in one. "I have reason to believe that the agents as a whole... are doing all they can, by refusing food until the Indians are on the verge of starvation, to reduce the expense," Macdonald told the House of Commons in 1882. How many Indigenous people died because basic needs including food, access to hunting, and the ability to move about to find food were restricted under his rule?

Recent debates about maintaining and revering statues are superficial. Should we keep the statues or not? The real issue is about what lessons we want to uphold in this country. So, yes, let's keep the statue and educate Canadians that it embodies all that is white supremacy in Canada. The minister of death, right here.

The worst of times

Moving on with this rapid tour of Canada's history. The early 1900s were the worst of times. There were numerous amendments to the Indian Act, truly horrific revisions. First Nations were restricted to their reserves, just like apartheid in South Africa, and jailed if they left those reserves. Food and medicine were at times withheld to force a First Nations community to comply with the Department of Indian Affairs. Police forces could be called in to enforce an Indian agent's will. Indigenous people were not allowed to wear their traditional clothing or regalia, unless given written approval by the Indian agent. However, approval was given for Indians to perform at the Calgary Stampede as entertainment, which is why this event has maintained such a long history for First Nations in the area. It was the only place that the old dances were allowed to be performed.

Moving on... it was illegal for Indigenous people to go into pool halls. It was illegal for Indians to gather in groups of more than four. It was illegal to hire a lawyer to fight against the removal of our rights. It was illegal for a lawyer to represent First Nations. It was illegal to practice the knowledge systems and cultures that had maintained us for thousands and thousands of years.

There were many policies and laws enacted to keep Indigenous people down, and they worked hand in hand with the residential schools policy. The TRC's Final Report was difficult for the country to take in, so this is a warning that the TRC was not able to tell the full story in 2015. The Office of the Independent Special Interlocutor for Missing Children and Unmarked Graves and Burial Sites associated with Indian Residential Schools released its findings in October 2024, and it is a brutal read. Ministers of Indian Affairs across decades have overseen the deaths of children in church-run institutions. So much so that these institutions always had graveyards next to them. Now we know that children died in the thousands due to neglect. There is clear evidence that babies and children were killed and buried in unmarked graves. Survivors have always known the truth, but somehow the federal government has kept it hidden from Canadians. Children were moved from institution to institution and intentionally disappeared

We are doing reconciliation in Canada because of the criminal acts done to Indigenous people in the past, and to fix the systems that still don't serve them well today.

from their families. The shocking truth, on top of this all, is that the federal government has politely given itself amnesty for all the crimes. No bureaucrat who wrote the memos about children dying has been charged. No political leader who said "this is how it's always been done" has been jailed. To be clear, governments that do this kind of criminal activity are charged and usually convicted in an international court of law.

Indigenous communities were probably wondering if they would survive. Many people did not, and we will probably never know how many thousands died by starvation, disease, conflict, and neglect in residential schools. We don't know how many Indigenous people lived prior to contact in what is now Canada, but the estimate is about 54 million across North America. It is possible that by the 1920s, less than half of the population here in Canada remained, possibly only one-third.

Everything started to change with World War II. When Germany committed genocide and then lost the war, the international community through the new United Nations said, never again will we allow a group to persecute and kill another group. The Universal Declaration of Human Rights was signed by hundreds of countries around the world in 1948. It protects our right to practice any religion, our right to vote in secret, our right to associate with whomever we want. Canada did not want to sign this document for many reasons, one of which was that the residential schools were in full swing at that time and policy leaders knew that stealing children would be seen as a violation of the Universal Declaration of Human Rights (therefore, they knew residential schools were wrong). At that time, Indigenous people had to be enfranchised to get the right to vote, so most didn't vote. Indigenous people were not considered voting citizens of Canada, right from the beginning of the country. A 1934 law explicitly disqualified Inuit from the right to vote. However, the Universal Declaration of Human Rights and the weight of international peer pressure fell on Canada, which signed on in the end, and things started to change for Indigenous people.

The operative word here is "started." It started to change. Canada did a peculiar move during the negotiation of the United Nations Declaration of Human Rights. A definition of genocide was declared and countries were expected to mirror the definition in domestic law, and many did so in order to protect the rights of all humans. Canada did not. Canada did a peculiar move to omit "cultural genocide" from the international definition, as if it was trying to cover its behind. As if it was trying to cover up what it was doing at that very time to Indigenous people. Imagine that. Flash forward to 2015 when Canada said residential schools could be considered cultural genocide, but not the real thing? Now it all makes sense.

Indigenous people could finally choose to go university and remain Indigenous instead of giving up their rights in exchange for enfranchisement. By 1960 all Indigenous people had the right to vote—a fundamental right of citizenship in a country. Indigenous communities started to hire lawyers to argue in court to embed their rights and ensure those rights were protected. Indigenous people went to school to be lawyers.

The civil rights movement of the 1960s in the United States was influential. Indigenous leaders travelled to the southern states to learn from leaders of the civil rights movement about their peaceful approach. There are many other countries in which the majority population has erased the minority population's rights, and quite honestly, civil war is the result. At some point a significant decision must have been made, because national Indigenous leaders continued to fight for their rights in a peaceful way in court. For the next decades, the struggle for rights and recognition was fought in courtrooms in many, many cases against Canada.

Recent history

Skip forward to the summer of 1990 in Oka, located west of Montreal. There was a long-standing oral agreement about a piece of land, sacred land between the municipality of Oka and the neighbouring First Nations community of Kanesatake. The municipality agreed to protect the agreement. A new municipal mayor was elected and decided the oral agreement was not his cup of tea. He wanted a golf course, and too quickly the machines were going in to level that sacred forest to make way for new development. The women of the First Nation stood in a line to stop the development and asked to negotiate. Sad story in Canada: when white people come out to march for or against something, it is called a demonstration, but when Indigenous people march, it is called a blockade. In one of the worst policing decisions in Canada's history since the war against Louis Riel, the provincial police of Quebec showed up in full tactical gear to force the "blockaders" to make way for graders. Things got so heated during the seventy-eight-day standoff that the Canadian military was sent in to try to keep people from hurting each other. A number of lessons come out of the Oka Crisis.

It was the first time that average Canadians saw Indigenous people on the nightly news, and it created all sorts of uncomfortable conversations around the dinner table. Unfortunately, mainstream media did not cover some nasty side stories happening around the crisis. As the days of the Oka Crisis turned into weeks, the provincial police blockaded First Nations people into place without water or food. Indigenous people from all across North America came to support the rights of the First Nation to their sacred land, and some smuggled in food and water at night. When Indigenous people returned in the early morning from the food runs, they reported being stoned as they crossed bridges back into Montreal. The Oka Crisis might have brought that vast gap between Indigenous people and settlers to the forefront, but it did not raise awareness about the blatant racism.

The Oka Crisis prompted uncomfortable questions like, Why are First Nations still fighting for their land? Why did the police respond with so much force instead of governments responding to talk? How did it get so bad? The Canadian government created the Royal Commission on Aboriginal Peoples to answer those questions. It's essential reading for the ally.

People started to ask questions, and Indigenous people who were willing to share were sometimes heard. One person who was heard was the then–National Chief of the Assembly of First Nations, Phil Fontaine. He spoke in a keynote address about how history continues to impact current-day relations between Indigenous and non-Indigenous Canadians. He also spoke about his residential school experience and the abuses he endured, and it was the first time that a public Indigenous figure spoke about abuse in those schools. His vulnerability gave courage to numerous survivors of residential schools to share their stories. The door had been opened.

The 1990s was also a time of hundreds of court cases. It could take sometimes ten to thirty years for a court case started by Indigenous communities to wind its way through to the Supreme Court, primarily because all levels of government fought against Indigenous people on almost every single case. One that finally made it to court was a class-action settlement by residential school survivors. At that time, such a huge class-action settlement had never been poised to go to court in Canada. In quiet negotiations with Indigenous leaders, the federal government agreed to settle out of court rather than proceed to trial. The settlement led to the Truth and Reconciliation Commission. Flash forward again to 2015, when the TRC tabled its Final Report and released its 94 Calls to Action at an emotional event in Ottawa.

It is said that Canada entered into its era of reconciliation in 2015. I'm not entirely sure that is the case. In 2015, too many Canadians still believed residential schools were a benevolent act on the behalf of the federal government to better Indigenous people's lives. Too many Canadians believed that Great Canadian Lie that it was in Indigenous people's best interest for their kids to be stolen into institutions.

We entered into reconciliation for real when news of searches for unmarked graves at those institutions for children began.

Road maps for reconciliation

We are doing reconciliation in Canada because of the criminal acts done to Indigenous people in the past. We are doing reconciliation in Canada because there is really no other way to get past it all, except to tell the truth and change the systems so that it never can happen again.

We have road maps on this journey of reconciliation: the United Nations Declaration on the Rights of Indigenous Peoples and the final reports of the TRC, the National Inquiry into Missing and Murdered Indigenous Women and Girls, and the Office of the Independent Special Interlocutor for Missing Children and Unmarked Graves and Burial Sites associated with Indian Residential Schools. But these road maps will have no meaning or value until we can ditch the Great Canadian Lie.

No, Indigenous people do not want to be dependent or deferential. No, Indigenous people are not inferior. No, Canada is not built on the two solitudes of English and French only. No, Indigenous Peoples have not been erased.

Canada is on Indigenous land. Canada is an Indigenous country. And Indigenous people hold knowledges and experiences on this land that are inherently central to this country.

NEXT STEPS

Choose to deepen your knowledge about Canada's history. Pick at least one resource from the list below and work through it. Give yourself the grace to be open to learning more.

Talk to a friend or work peer about what was new for you and what it was like for you to integrate that new knowledge into your thoughts, because this is how you give grace to others to be open to learning more.

Do research on where the closest residential school to you was located, how many children might have attended, and if Indigenous communities have chosen to search for unmarked graves.

RESOURCES

Joseph, Bob. *21 Things You May Not Know About the Indian Act: Helping Canadians Make Reconciliation with Indigenous Peoples a Reality*. Indigenous Relations Press, 2018.

Obomsawin, Alanis. *Kanehsatake: 270 Years of Resistance*. 1993. Available to watch in Canada from the National Film Board website (nfb.ca).

Standing Senate Committee on Aboriginal Peoples. *How Did We Get Here? A Concise, Unvarnished Account of the History of the Relationship Between Indigenous Peoples and Canada.* Interim Report, April 2019.

Talaga, Tanya. *The Knowing.* HarperCollins, 2024.

Truth and Reconciliation Commission of Canada. *They Came for the Children: Canada, Aboriginal Peoples, and Residential Schools.* 2012.

3

CHALLENGING INTERPERSONAL RACISM

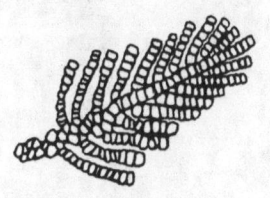

No one is born hating another person because of the color of his skin, or his background, or his religion. People must learn to hate, and if they can learn to hate, they can be taught to love, for love comes more naturally to the human heart than its opposite.

NELSON MANDELA

Humans do better at life when we choose to learn from others who have different cultures and ways of seeing and experiencing the world. Foundational to championing diversity and inclusion in our communities and at work is valuing the learning that others gift to us. But racism creates barriers for relationship and learning between people and between neighbours. Racism diminishes us all.

On a brisk evening in Toronto in 2019, I had the misfortune of slipping on black ice and falling with all the awkwardness of a deer on a frozen lake. I fractured my wrist and ended up at Michael Garron Hospital. Thankfully, I was with a First Nations friend who took me to the hospital. We joked on the way, "Gee, I hope we actually get treated." It's the kind of cynical humour that is sometimes shared between Indigenous friends who have experienced too much racism in hospitals. When I walked into the urban hospital's emergency room, the admitting nurse saw me immediately and waved me over for prompt service. Within minutes, I was into the triage room, where the triage nurse treated me with so such respect. She never doubted that I was in pain. Within minutes again the doctor was over to start treatment, and he recognized that I was First Nations and offered to connect me with the hospital's Elder. I was treated and out the door in hours.

I share this story because it was the first time I had been in an emergency room and had not faced racism but felt truly respected and supported. True story. This was the first time that I was not ignored. I was not dismissed. I was not assumed to be drunk. My pain was not doubted. My culture was not seen as a detriment. Note that I have not experienced all of those racist factors in a single emergency room visit, but I have experienced them all at different points in different hospitals. I look like I am First Nations and I cannot hide it, so I am at risk of racism every time I have to enter a hospital for myself or with my family.

That night at Michael Garron Hospital, I was in disbelief. Do white Canadians experience that kind of safety in hospitals? I want to experience that every time. I need to feel safe in emergency rooms, as does every single

Indigenous individual. Indigenous people deserve to feel safe, free from interpersonal racism, free from being given less service or being targeted because of culture, free from hurtful stereotypes. Racism is a disease that risks the lives of Indigenous people, and racism within healthcare simply reflects the wider issue.

There are too many stories about how systems treat Indigenous people differently.

Indigenous people in Canada are assumed to be poor, uneducated, unemployed, and/or drunk. In the healthcare system, when healthcare providers act on their biases, Indigenous people wait longer and receive poorer-quality services than others. When this happens, we inside First Nations communities call it the invisibility syndrome: providers simply do not see us in the admitting rooms and in the hallways. From reports in the city of Ottawa, British Columbia, Alberta, and more, about three-quarters of Indigenous people who had to go into urban hospitals and mainstream healthcare systems faced racism by healthcare workers.

But racism against Indigenous people is a risk and problem beyond the healthcare sector.

After the tragic loss of George Floyd at the hands of police officers in Minneapolis, Minnesota, on May 25, 2020, the word "racism" finally started to be used regularly in Canadian conversations. Allies in Canada learned more about the inequitable treatment that Black Canadians endured here, joined Black Lives Matter

Racism is the disease that threatens the soul of reconciliation.

marches, and talked about how we stop racism. Allies needed to show their support for Black Canadians and need to continue to do so, no question. Allies are an essential element in changing societal norms and myths, one of which is that Canada is multicultural and equitable. I hope this does not come as a surprise, but Canada isn't really multicultural and equitable. Canada treats people of colour differently, and Canada has enshrined laws to treat Indigenous people as less-than.

Canada has always treated Indigenous people differently from white Canadians—so much so that the inequity could be considered part of the country's fabric. If you want to change this, then you have to talk about racism and then do something about racism. If racism continues to be a deadly disease impacting Indigenous people, then it will be difficult to talk about reconciliation with authenticity.

In the first six months of 2020, the same year that George Floyd died, several Indigenous Canadians died at the hands of police—an Inuk artist in Ottawa, another Inuk in Nunavut, three Indigenous individuals in three different incidents in Winnipeg in a span of ten days, a First Nations woman in New Brunswick, and another First Nations person in that same province. Yet these deaths did not spark outrage in Canadians and scarcely even received media coverage. Did they deserve to be killed? The answer is no. One of these individuals was the subject of a mental health check, Canada's worst-kept secret related to police being called to check in on somebody with perceived mental health challenges. The loss of this individual at the hands of people who were supposed to care for her is horrible.

Nobody tracks deaths at the hands of police, but journalists in 2020 through an "access-to-information request revealed more than a third of people shot to death by RCMP officers between 2007 and 2017 were Indigenous, despite Indigenous people only making up 5 per cent of the population." Since 2017, an Indigenous person in Canada is more than ten times more likely than a white person to be shot and killed by a police officer in Canada. When one racial group disproportionately endures police brutality more than another, that is the definition of institutional racism—treating one group differently across a whole system.

I face the risk of racism while shopping for clothes in nicer stores as I'm assumed to be First Nations and therefore broke and a thief. It happens to me at least two or three times a year. Or somebody assumes I can't possibly own my house because it's too nice. Or assumes that I can't possibly own my vehicle because aren't all First Nations people broke? It's all racism, and this is the daily interpersonal racism that needs to be eradicated like a disease. Racism is the disease that threatens the soul of reconciliation.

Racism on a systems or institutional level can be measured. The proportion of Indigenous people who sit on big corporate boards or hospital boards is so small that the number is hard to count. The proportion of Indigenous people in CEO and VP positions is growing but is still smaller than the proportion of the population. If racism were not a problem, we would see proportions of Indigenous people in these positions equivalent to proportions of Indigenous people in the overall population—about 5 percent. Anything less requires us to ask, Why? What are the barriers? How is racism not a barrier?

I recognize this is a big ask, for you to open your eyes to the racism that Indigenous people experience in Canada. It is a big ask because once you open your eyes, you won't be able to close your eyes again to the problem. You might see it on public transit, on buses and subways, as staff assume an Indigenous person has not paid the fare. You might see it on the streets, as police assume Indigenous people must be dangerous simply because they are Indigenous. You might see far too many instances in which a healthcare or service provider does not give the benefit of the doubt to an Indigenous individual and makes snap judgements. Or in municipalities that forget to respect the National Day for Truth and Reconciliation. Or when authorities forget to include Indigenous communities in the emergency response to wildfires. Racism is in the action that gives lower-quality services to an individual and in a lack of compassion in the face of need.

Step in to stop racism

An interesting thing happens when an Indigenous individual experiencing racism steps up in self-defence: the situation gets worse. Apparently Indigenous people are supposed to stay quiet and subservient but never get angry. An Indigenous patient asserting the right to equitable treatment for themselves in a hospital might risk a security response, but a white Canadian would likely not receive this response. A white Canadian who wants good treatment or service and voices that request (or demand) is likely to be heard and given the benefit of the doubt even if they are angry. A white Canadian can generally ask a police officer why the officer is doing what they are doing and receive an answer. Indigenous people who ask questions might end up on the ground. That's how racism goes in Canada. The benefit of the doubt is rarely given to Indigenous people.

How do you stop racism? Take responsibility as an essential part of the community you want to help. You step in to stop it. Be the ally, right here and right now.

Allies committed to contributing to reconciliation have a large and essential role. When witnessing racism, allies must step up and step in. It is unfair to expect Indigenous people, or any group who is at risk of racism, to challenge racism while they are being victimized by it. More often than not, an ally has much more influence and ability to intervene than Indigenous individuals. What would it take for you to move from being a bystander to being an actor in a situation where you witness an Indigenous individual experiencing racism?

What would it look like for you to take those two small steps from bystander to actor? I would like you to consider that you have a choice. Do you choose to step in? Adults tend to do better when they *choose* rather than simply *react*. When you choose to do something, your cognition balances your emotion, and you are more likely to slow things down for everybody. So choose to step in. Think about a first line that you might use to slow down a whole event for the people involved. It does not have to be a gold-star-level intervention, but you do need to slow the event down. You might say something as simple as, "I don't understand what's happening here. Can I help?" The next step is to consider how you can call in the individual who said or did something racist to do better.

Have you heard of the phrase "call in"? You've likely heard "call out." The phrase and action to "call out" unacceptable behaviour has a sense of confrontation, but the phrase and action of "calling in" unacceptable behaviour is based in a key value of believing an individual can choose to do better. Approach difficult conversations with the belief that individuals can learn more to do better. If you give yourself this grace, you can also give others this grace.

Keep in mind that challenging racism is one of the most difficult conversations to have in a workplace, but this is where there are codes of conduct and expectations of professionalism. Rely on and uphold those codes for civil discourse, as workplaces are where we codify what we want in society writ large. And then try this approach: "It's all practice." If you let go of the expectation that you will model a perfect intervention in a racist incident, you reduce the pressure on yourself. It truly is all practice. The moment you choose to step in, you've already influenced the situation for the better.

If you choose to intervene in an instance of racism, always keep as your top goal the safety of the people involved as well as your own safety. There may be instances of racism that are truly not safe to intervene in. Use your judgement and be aware. The whole point of stepping in and calling in unacceptable behaviour is to increase safety for all.

In the majority of instances of racism against Indigenous people, it is safe for bystanders to intervene, and that is the role for allies. It may feel uncomfortable. In teaching adults from across Canada how to challenge racism, I have heard from many allies that challenging racism is daunting, intimidating, unnerving. Let's be honest, this is one of the most challenging conversations that you might choose to have. But the fact that a conversation might be challenging is not a good reason to walk away. And I guarantee you, you will not be nearly as uncomfortable as the Indigenous individual who is experiencing racism.

I have asked you to step up and challenge racism for a few key reasons. The first is that, as already discussed, it's too much to ask a person experiencing racism to also try to educate a perpetrator. The second is that there are always other people watching and silence will be seen as support, so do not be seen as supporting racism by doing nothing. Another reason is modelling: people will be watching you and learning about how you challenge racism, so model the kind of behaviour and community that you want, be it at work or in your family or in your neighbourhood. The last reason is regret. I have taught thousands and thousands of Canadians from coast to coast to coast how to challenge racism, and invariably, in every class, a learner shares about a time when they witnessed racism and did not do anything. The tone of their voice as they share about that experience reflects the depth of regret they continue to feel years after the incident.

Here is a recipe for stepping in: Choose to step in for safety. Take a calming breath and catch the eye of another bystander who will most likely back you up. Say your line that interrupts and slows down the racist incident. Gently move in to stand beside the Indigenous individual and catch their eye to see if they are okay.

And then it depends on the response of the individual who did or said something unacceptable. Focus on the behaviour—in community, we have the right to demand behaviour changes. But we can't demand an individual to change. This is a key difference—always focus on the behaviour that must change. More often than not, adults hate being critiqued in public and the individual will back down. Rarely, the individual may dig in, and you might have to speak plainly about the unacceptable behaviour.

Challenging "but I didn't mean it" racism

I am not sure if this is a Canadian thing, but can we please stop saying "but I didn't mean it" to avoid taking responsibility? The scenario usually plays out like this. A behaviour or comment is named as racist, and the person dodges by saying the easy out, "I didn't mean it." Except that is not a way out; it is a blatant refusal to take responsibility.

To paraphrase the expert facilitator Lisa Zimmerman, if there were a pile of plates on a table, and as I walked past, I knocked them off and one fell on your foot and hurt you, then as an adult I must take responsibility for the impact of my actions on you. I am not responsible for what is bumping around in my head, but I am responsible for the effect of my actions on you. Good intent is how you imagine seeing yourself doing something, but the impact of what you do is always what matters. If I hurt you, I have to make amends and clean up my mess.

If you choose to intervene with an individual who acted on racism and receive the response "but I didn't mean it," ask them how this takes responsibility for their impact on others.

Challenging "it's just one bad apple" racism

When an incident of racism occurs in plain sight, there is a good chance someone will try the "bad apples" claim. For example, let's picture an incident in which a police officer somehow physically assaults an Indigenous individual without provocation, and it is captured on video. Police unions and fellow police officers might say, "He's just a bad apple." What does that mean? The response is an immoral attempt to say that the attacker's fellow police officers are not culpable or accountable for the actions of their peer. The response is a blatant attempt to avoid collective responsibility, but it's worse than that. The bad-apple response is a complete dodge of responsibility. It suggests that a singular instance of racism is a one-off and does not matter, is rare, and is not a pattern. It's just that guy. In essence, the bad-apple claim is an attempt to say, "We're not racist. Just that person is, and just this one time so let it go." The racist behaviour is buried by rhetoric and goes unpunished.

The bad-apple claim is pervasive, even when an Indigenous person is hurt or dies by racism. But there's another saying that "one bad apple can spoil the bunch."

Even if an incident is the result of the actions of just one or two individuals, it is one or two too many and risks our shared sense of safe community. Does anybody seriously want to let the one or two off the hook for perpetuating racism? Bad apples are rarely punished for the potential crimes, because systems protect them by using the bad-apple response. If a situation is caused by just a few bad apples, then I don't have to do anything, do I? This argument turns out to be the perfect way to prop up a system that allows racism. (We'll talk more about systems in the next chapter.)

The bad-apple approach just doesn't fly. We would not, as a society, allow a few bad apples to be airline pilots, would we? We should not, as a society, allow a few bad apples in any profession, especially for those who are expected to treat others with equity. This is a horrible way to diminish the experience of the victimized.

The lack of compassion for the Indigenous individual who may have been hurt in this instance is truly appalling. The truth is that there are not just a few bad apples. Racism against Indigenous people happens every day, in policing, in healthcare, in child welfare, on the street. Canada baked racism into its systems, and no one would like to be on the receiving end of it.

In response to the bad-apple excuse, ask, "How are you taking responsibility for your impact?" Get ready to say, "The bad-apple approach is not acceptable here; we need you to do better." Demand people take responsibility for good behaviour of the team. Choose to step in. Choose to call in a bad-apple response. Adults are expected to be responsible for their impact on others. We demand better from one another. We all have a role to play to maintain our community.

Challenging "blame the victim" racism

The "blame the victim" response is pretty nasty. Something bad happens to an Indigenous individual, and others say it's that person's fault and, in so doing, absolve themselves of any responsibility to care. The basis to the argument that an Indigenous individual "deserved it" or "just doesn't want any better" is the belief that an individual of that race/culture is less worthy and has fewer rights. It is the very essence of racism. And this happens quite regularly in Canada, especially when we add on another layer such as homelessness or mental health challenges. Then we hear it too often about Indigenous individuals: "It's their fault they're homeless." Or "they just won't make better choices" when Indigenous people use drugs or alcohol. Racism, when combined with stigma of another issue, becomes life-threatening, as it can rationalize a lack of response in the face of need, a lack of action for neighbours in our communities who most need the help. It is racism on steroids.

How can bystanders step in when they witness this type of racism? Ask the individual who is saying these types of things, "What evidence leads you to believe that person deserves less?" Or "What would you say if that person were my sister or brother?"

Why it starts with you

Some might argue that challenging this interpersonal racism on the streets or in the workplace won't fix the real problem—the big systemic racism built into this country. Why do something about a small racist incident at work when there are huge societal issues for Indigenous people?

Let's return to a change management approach for this. Change management—whether it's about an organizational chart shift in a company, a new strategic plan in an organization, or a big societal change in a country—functions in similar patterns: Name the problem and build consensus that it is a priority problem to fix now. Name a solution and build buy-in for it. Support people to change and do things differently. Celebrate the change.

In a change management approach, we start with individuals and support them to change. Then the system starts to reflect the people. Systems reflect us. We are the change.

If you challenge racism against Indigenous people in your daily life, you will start to shift what is acceptable in your community, network, or workplace. When you start to shift what is acceptable in your local setting, the social more that you choose to uphold of no more racism spreads as others also start to call in racism. As more and more Canadians demand better from one another, the systems will start to change to reflect the determination to treat people equitably. That's how you change whole systems—you change and you support those around you to change.

Workplaces are where we codify behaviours that we want to see in society: civility, fairness, equity, inclusion. Workplaces are incredibly important microcosms of wider society, and they are also the agent of change for a society. This is the fulcrum of change in Canada—your workplace. If we can enact reconciliation here, then we normalize it across society. If we don't embed reconciliation here, it will not happen anywhere else. Codify it. Put anti-racism in your organization's code of conduct; write down your expectations for inclusion in procedure.

But if you do not stop racism on the streets, you will not be able to change your community, workplace, society, or systems. In other words, stopping racism is local action in your community, network, and workplace. We start building belonging and community here.

This is possible. You need to know that it is possible. Racism is a learned behaviour and belief. So if children show care and compassion to each other regardless of race, we as adults can question biases that we've picked up along the way, choose to drop those biases, and choose to be respectful of others.

I often wonder what it would be like to walk through my life without fear of racism. I often wonder just how much of my stress is composed of that fear. What would I be like without that stress? What would Indigenous youth be like without that stress load? Would we laugh more? Would we take up more space? Would we anticipate respect, even look forward to it, maybe even believe in it?

Of course we would. That's a glimpse of what it could look like when we do reconciliation as a country.

—— NEXT STEPS ——

Consider a hypothetical incident of racism against an Indigenous individual and practice out loud what you might say. You're standing in line behind an Indigenous individual at a coffee shop, and the server obviously ignores the Indigenous person and turns to you. What would you say? Come up with four different lines you could say to step in.

Work through this scenario with a close friend or co-worker. Allies bring their personal experiences to the table and might have different ways of approaching this. Hearing what others might do is a learning opportunity.

—— RESOURCES ——

Grenny, Joseph, Kerry Patterson, Ron McMillan, Al Switzler, and Emily Gregory. *Crucial Conversations: Tools for Talking when Stakes Are High.* 3rd ed. McGraw Hill, 2021.

Nowak, Anita. *Purposeful Empathy: Tapping Our Hidden Superpower for Personal, Organizational, and Social Change.* Augsburg Fortress Publishers, 2023.

4

CHALLENGING INSTITUTIONAL RACISM

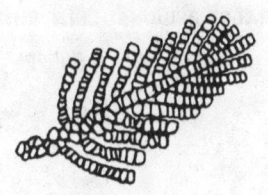

Numerous studies have confirmed that First Nations people are more likely to be detained by the police following an arrest, most often on the basis of prejudice and racism. They are also more likely to be detained for long periods of time as part of the bail process. They are more likely to be sentenced to imprisonment and, too often, for long periods. They are more likely to be imprisoned for non-payment of fines.

QUEBEC/LABRADOR REGIONAL CHIEF GHISLAIN PICARD,
Assembly of First Nations

IN THE previous chapter, we talked about incidents of interpersonal racism, incidents between individuals treating others differently because of race or culture, such as giving less service or no service in retail, hospitals, or hotels. Interpersonal racism is putting the belief into action that your race or culture is somehow less worthy than mine.

Institutional racism is when whole systems reflect bias against a minority or pass laws specifically for a minority, such as the Indian Act. Or policies that give differential access, such as Indigenous healthcare funding that is segregated from the rest of Canada and then funded less. When institutional racism is allowed to continue for long enough, it seems almost impossible for those who want to, to do better. It's like the system is so strong that it's impossible to imagine a different future. The force of the status quo is so beyond interrogation that it seems like it is the only way. Does Canada have a problem with institutional racism? Yes, Canada does it quite well. The secret to changing institutional racism is to recognize it and then to apply astute pressure and influence to overcome the force of "status quo-ism."

The racism faced by Indigenous people in Canada is difficult to deconstruct, as it is both generations old and propped up by law. Remember the Indian Act? It is a criminal piece of legislation that governs the lives of Indigenous people in this country, and it is so offensive that it could not be passed into law today. But the country has had this law on the books for generations, and so it is difficult to imagine a future without it. There have been serious attempts to dismantle the act, and some of the loudest voices against change have been bureaucrats within the Department of Indian Affairs (at the time of writing called Crown-Indigenous Relations and Northern Affairs), which along with Indigenous Services Canada today constitutes the federal government's largest department. You can almost hear the proclamations from civil servants. "What would the Indigenous communities do without us?"

At the crux of the mess is this: it's a myth that Indigenous people want the Indian Act or want to remain wards of the state. There is a strong taint of "blame the victim" racism here, the most jarring racism of all. As long as this horrible and racist myth continues, that Indigenous people do not want something better or different, there's no motivation to change anything. There is no need to address the inequitable funding for First Nations families and children stuck in child welfare, no urgency to fix the thousands of houses filled with mould, no use in questioning why there are still emergencies of lack of clean water in Indigenous communities. When we blame the victim and think that it's because Indigenous people can't maintain water systems, or won't parent better or can't, then it becomes so easy to default to the Great Canadian Lie: "We're doing our best."

This monumental, legislated racism created the monster of residential schools, along with policies and laws that rationalized fewer services and less funding for First Nations citizens compared to "real" citizens who deserve the best we can afford. And it continues. Government of Canada offices are stacked from floor to ceiling with briefing notes and rationales about why nothing can really change, despite numerous protestations and calls for justice from Indigenous people themselves. "Fund us equitably as you do the rest of Canada" is the mantra from Indigenous communities, and this demand sparks a forceful resistance from the government.

"We won't fund this group of Canadians the way we fund this other group of Canadians because it costs too much." Can you imagine a government saying this out loud? This is institutional racism, to pay less for the same services for Indigenous people—racism baked into systems so completely that it is difficult to fight. In contrast, for example, if the federal government gave one province 30 percent more money per capita for hospitals, all hell would break loose from the other provinces and territories. It would not be seen as fair; it would not be seen as constitutional.

Worse, governments underfund Indigenous people's systems on your behalf, and in essence assume that you don't want your taxes to go to Indigenous people equitably. As a taxpayer, I find it particularly galling that the federal government thinks it's doing this for me too.

As a side note, Indigenous people pay income tax, gas tax, HST, property taxes off-reserve—we pay them all, just as other Canadians do. A small number of First Nations individuals who live and work on-reserve for First Nations–owned companies and governments do not pay income tax.

Racism and funding inequities

Let's talk about water as an example of racism and funding inequities.

As I write this, Calgary is frantically fixing a water pipe that supplies more than half of the city's water. City officials are pleading with Calgarians to reduce their water use, because they may run out of water. It is an "all hands on deck" emergency. I do not mean to make light of the seriousness of the situation in Calgary, but let's keep this in perspective. There are tens and tens of Indigenous communities without clean drinking water, and Canadians have never been "all hands on deck" for these communities.

It is worth digging into this issue as an example of how Indigenous communities continue to face wide inequities related to basic needs that most Canadians take for granted.

Clean water is a responsibility of the municipality for most Canadians. Almost all Canadians pay for clean water, along with sewer wastewater treatment, through municipal taxes and/or provincial taxes. This covers the hundreds of kilometres of pipes in any given town, the treatment of water, the treatment of wastewater, all the related equipment, and the professionals who maintain the systems. In much of Canada, the infrastructure for cities was built during the massive building boom of the 1960s, and the cost to maintain aging infrastructure is increasing. It is difficult to estimate an average cost of water for a household in the country, because each town and city might tax differently. A very rough average might be $2.50 per cubic metre of water, but city fees vary widely. A household in Thunder Bay, Ontario, might pay about $1,300 per year, while a household in Vancouver might pay about $800 per year.

In First Nations reserves, the federal government (Indigenous Services Canada) is responsible for funding water systems. As you've seen in the news, water systems are a crisis with tens and tens of boil-water advisories. Moms go out numerous times a day to a river or lake with pails to get water and then boil it, or planes fly in bottled water to remote communities. In some communities there may be pipes in the ground to supply water, but the treatment plant is so old that the water has to be boiled. Or the reverse may be true, with a working water treatment plant but no pipes to connect homes. The building boom of infrastructure that occurred in cities decades ago did not occur in First Nations communities. Some communities have no infrastructure at all; some have failed treatment plants because of lack of parts or servicing.

In 2015, the Liberal government committed to eliminating 133 boil-water advisories by March 2021. Yes, 133 advisories. More than one hundred communities in Canada in 2015 couldn't drink the water. The federal government allocated some $2 billion into clean drinking water for First Nations in 2016–17, and it sounded like big money. But just as in Canadian towns and cities, there are capital, or infrastructure, costs (laying pipe, building water treatment centres), and there are costs for ongoing maintenance of those systems (fixing pipes, paying salaries of water professionals). In 2017 and in 2021, the Office of the Parliamentary Budget Officer, the trustworthy auditor of federal spending, looked into Indigenous Services Canada's funding for clean drinking water and found glaring gaps. In 2017, the Parliamentary Budget Officer "found that the total historical spending since 2011–2012 and planned spending announced in Budget 2016 would only cover between 50 and 70 per cent of the total investment needs of First Nations [water and wastewater] infrastructure." The federal government is prone to making media announcements about seemingly big money, but they know that amount won't fix the issue. It's a band-aid.

By 2021, the federal government had not even come close to eliminating all boil-water advisories for First Nations—there were still forty-four advisories. That's about the number of communities who heard all the COVID advice to wash their hands but had no water taps, or the water they could access was so contaminated that it caused skin issues. In the last few years, the Budget Officer believes the funding is enough for infrastructure needs but not for the ongoing operations, and notes that the $4.3 billion to be spent over the next couple of years is not enough to cover the real costs. "The historical spending since 2016–2017 and planned spending until 2025–2026 on [water and wastewater operation] and maintenance will only cover just over two thirds of funding needs." I know it sounds like big money, but imagine that $1,000 per household, when it all gets summed up across the province of Ontario with its 5.5 million households. This is the real and routine cost of clean water that democracies pay through taxation.

Because there has been so much lag by the federal government to fund the fixes required so that all First Nations have clean drinking water, the government has also been sued for the failure to take all reasonable steps to provide access to safe drinking water. The federal government is paying out a settlement totalling some $8 billion. That is a big number and it is also taxpayers' money, paid out because the federal government failed on something so basic as clean drinking water.

This example shows the kind of analysis needed to put the inequities in context. Virtually every single system from education to child welfare to healthcare to road maintenance in First Nations communities is still underfunded compared to what you receive in your city or town.

Think of it this way. Would you put up with your municipality or provincial or territorial government saying it's just too expensive to connect clean water for your whole neighbourhood or suburb? So why do we put up with your government saying it's too difficult and too expensive to connect your neighbouring First Nation community to clean water?

How systems can be forced to change

In terms of funding inequities, there is one actor that forces governments to do better: the court systems. Courts have forced the federal government to pay for its sins of neglect, such as immorally underfunding child welfare for First Nations, refusal to adequately address the lack of clean water in a timely fashion, and more. In 2024, the tab passed $40 billion in the last few years, including a $23 billion settlement for historic and current underfunding in child welfare. Why is this important? When politicians refuse to serve all citizens equally in a democracy, at some point there is a substantial penalty to pay in redress. Canada and its taxpayers are now paying for the racism of inequitable funding and neglect. Yet, Government of Canada lawyers, on the direction of bureaucrats and politicians, are fighting even today against lawsuits from Indigenous communities for equitable services. Whole systems of governments need to change to reflect the values of reconciliation and equity; otherwise, the courts will continue to force large compensation packages. Perhaps somebody should do something about governments still living like it's the 1960s.

In public policy and governing, there's "upstream" and "downstream." Upstream are the things that citizens all deserve such as water, healthcare, safe policing, all the institutions and services in functioning democracies.

Downstream are the impacts on people and communities that functioning systems protect: good health outcomes, safe communities, opportunities to thrive. In functioning democracies, the upstream institutions and services are supposed to treat everybody equitably. Here's the kicker in Canada. When racism is baked into the systems so that Indigenous people are funded less and possibly treated with racism, then there are downstream impacts. Indigenous people face more risk of illness and all sorts of other downstream impacts. The statistics say that Indigenous people are at higher risks of mental illness, chronic disease, and death at the hands of police. Any statistic in Canada that shows that Indigenous people are doing worse than non-Indigenous people is actually a measure of the failure of the institutions and services.

Every culture has value; no society or culture is better or worse than any other. No society, people, or culture has some innate genetic deficit or is somehow "less than" another. No culture or race is "better than." Therefore, if one minority culture or group in a country endures a higher rate of disease or incarceration or murder than another, then the system is treating those people differently. It's not like they're all genetically inferior or something, right? When one group is funded differently than another in Canada, we have a problem that requires Canadians to care.

What can allies do to change these institutionally racist systems? As we talked about in the previous chapter,

We are attempting to build community and society in which Indigenous people belong.

the first step is to stop racism around you, to step in. The next step is to deepen your education about current inequities for Indigenous people and imagine what needs to be done to fix the inequities. Don't give in to the Great Canadian Lie that this is how it's always been, so it will always be. Next-level allies also step in with friends, family, and networks to educate them on the Great Canadian Lie, so that they also challenge the racist assumptions. And then citizens start to challenge those in governments and in politics to do better for Indigenous people. That's how change happens.

Are we attempting to change the course of history in this country? History tends to be told by the victors, not by the oppressed. Did you hear about how the women's vote was fought for and won in 1918 but excluded Indigenous women, or that the massive infrastructure boom of the 1960s did not touch Indigenous communities? I took a world history class in university and found Indigenous Peoples were deemed so lowly that their whole existence was only worth a paragraph in the huge textbook. A paragraph. When I brought this blatant omission to the instructor, I found the jagged edge of a historian who took the time to correct my error and told me, "Indigenous Peoples don't show the hallmarks of civilization and what have they done anyways?"

It isn't history with the jagged edges. It is racism with the jagged edges that cut so deeply. Racism has many sharp edges to cut Indigenous people out from history, from equitable funding for health and well-being, from full inclusion in government priorities. Racism has kept Indigenous people out of the story in Canada now for generations. Attempts to overcome the exclusion and racism must surmount generations of stories that Canadians have told themselves.

We are attempting to change the course of racism. We are attempting to build community and society in which Indigenous people belong. Belonging is the opposite of exclusion and racism. Belonging is the hallmark of community.

The necessary step we must all take is to eradicate this very deadly disease of racism. This is the prerequisite for reconciliation. It starts with allies for Indigenous people, allies who take the time to question the historical myths of Canada, who choose to call in racism when they see it, and who take the time to call out governments who say they are acting in their name when they refuse equitable services and funding for Indigenous people. It's time.

NEXT STEPS

Learn more about the closest Indigenous community to you. How many people live in the community? What health services do they offer in the community? What police force is contracted? If people in the community need healthcare that is not offered in the community, where do they go? What's going well in the community?

Learn more about a remote fly-in Indigenous community in your province/territory. Research the same questions as above. Find out how much it costs to fly in or out of this community.

Find more than one Indigenous journalist or columnist, and commit to read their columns to continue to learn more about current issues facing Indigenous people.

RESOURCES

Lux, Maureen K. *Separate Beds: A History of Indian Hospitals in Canada, 1920s–1980s*. University of Toronto Press, 2016.

Walker, Connie, host. *Missing & Murdered: Finding Cleo*. CBC True Crime podcast. cbc.ca/radio/findingcleo.

Sinclair, Murray. *Who We Are: Four Questions for a Life and a Nation*. McClelland & Stewart, 2024.

Talaga, Tanya. *Seven Fallen Feathers: Racism, Death, and Hard Truths in a Northern City*. House of Anansi Press, 2017.

5

LENDING YOUR VOICE, INFLUENCE, AND PRIVILEGE

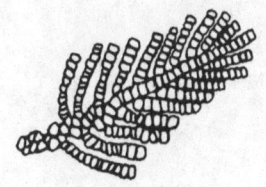

Empathy is the most powerful emotional force in the world, second only to love—especially if it's wielded on purpose… It increases our dopamine, reduces our stress, boosts our self-esteem, heightens our immune system, enriches our relationships, and even improves our key performance indicators at work.

ANITA NOWAK

BACK IN THE 1940s, Canada was an ally to England in World War II. It was such a strong bond that the international partners fighting against the Axis forces were called the Allied Powers. The word comes from the Latin word *alligare* meaning "to be bound to." The dictionary defines "ally" as a state bound by treaty, as well as a person "that is associated with another as a helper; a person or group that provides assistance and support in an ongoing activity or struggle."

Allies are those who lend their voices, influence, and privilege to support and amplify the goals of a marginalized group to which they do not belong. More recently, allies have been helpful in supporting causes important to Black people, Indigenous people, and other people of colour.

Destine Lord, a Black Canadian with roots from Trinidad and Tobago, is a well-known anti-racism leader based on the west coast. When she speaks about Black Lives Matter, she invariably speaks about Indigenous liberation too, and uses her voice to build solidarity between Black and Indigenous Canadians. Destine is an incredibly effective ally for reconciliation. When I asked her what makes an effective ally, Destine answered fairly quickly.

> An ally is not only about what you do... it's also about your core values for equity. How could anybody call themselves a proud Canadian when Indigenous people don't get equitable treatment? If you believe in human rights, you have to be an active ally for reconciliation. I can't believe we'd even question this. Allyship needs to be rooted in equity. Black and Indigenous folks have been calling for equitable approaches and solutions for years. People don't realize that the absence of equity impacts all of us. How could it not?

And yet the word "ally" sometimes sparks debate. Some do not like the word because people sometimes use it as a badge of honour, claiming "I am an ally" loudly from the mountaintops. Kind of ironic to proclaim to be an ally with all the privilege, maybe? Please do not proclaim to be an ally. Instead bring humility to the work.

Dr. Julie Cafley is the executive director of Catalyst Canada, an organization with a mandate to increase the number of women in executive roles as well as increasing diversity, inclusion, and equity in workforces. Julie is white with roots in Ireland and England, and generations of history in Ontario and Quebec. I call Julie an ally but she doesn't like the term.

> When you have privilege, I think the need to be an ally is really a non-question. You use the opportunities that you have to help, so why would you not? The term "ally" is frequently misunderstood. Frankly, I think there's a lot of performative allyship out there. You know, the empty words that signal you want to be seen as an ally but don't do anything to back that up. I believe the term "ally" is not something you can give yourself, it is only something that others can bestow on you.

Allyship is a verb, not a badge or gold star that you can give yourself. Allyship is earned and recognized in you by others. Allyship is skill, practice, and art, just like an athlete builds capacity for next-level sports.

We can look to several prominent examples of allyship in action.

On August 20, 2016, Gord Downie took the stage with the Tragically Hip for their nationally televised final show, and spoke about reconciliation to the audience and the country. Gord called on Canada to truly engage in reconciliation and to make amends for residential schools. What a great example of using your stage to amplify the messages of Indigenous people. He used his influence to move millions of people.

In 2016, Inuit were speaking out against the use of seismic testing underwater that they saw would harm sea life. They were struggling to get media attention, which is one way to get government leaders' attention, and then British actor Emma Thompson showed up. She lent her voice to the fight and suddenly this story was covered by media. Emma proved to be an effective ally.

Angie Seth is a well-known media anchor who chose to use her influence to amplify the stories of those impacted by racism in Canada. Angie was born in Winnipeg, Manitoba, with roots in northern India. When she anchored the evening news on CTV News Channel, she was well known for bringing forward stories about Indigenous people, both about racism and about the strengths of the people. Angie said allies in Canada for reconciliation need to bring "education, humility, and humanity." She did the work to understand what happened in history, reading the final reports of the TRC and the National Inquiry into Missing and Murdered Indigenous Women and Girls. She wanted to have enough understanding so that she would do no harm. Angie also exemplifies humility in the ways she shows respect for Indigenous people. Angie's advice to Canadians is to educate yourself, practice your humility, and bring humanity into everything. I can't help but think of Dr. Martin Luther King, Jr.'s words when I think of Angie.

> Make a career of humanity. Commit yourself to the noble struggle for equal rights. You will make a better person of yourself, a greater Nation of your country, and a finer world to live in.

How to become a next-level ally

What follows will be a lesson in Indigenous ways of being. You may have expected a checkbox or list here on what to do to be an effective ally in the next year, and the truth is that I will not give you a checklist. Let's talk about how you live your values as opposed to what you do, because this is how allies are evaluated.

Culture is a curious thing. We rarely talk about it in Canada, as if we all share the same culture. But we don't. We certainly share some values, but culturally we portray those values and act on those values differently. For example, we all value children. But compare a culture that values "children who are seen and not heard" to one that believes "children are the centre." And there you have it. We share a value but live it differently based at least partly on culture.

Here's another example: credibility. Culture underpins how we see, define, and measure credibility. Canadian culture defines credibility as what we do with job titles, accomplishments, and public visibility. And Indigenous people generally define it as who we are and how we live our values.

Credibility

Next-level allies practice their skill and art with a clear sense of protecting and building their credibility with Indigenous people and with other allies. Because being an ally is a team sport.

Credibility is earned in the world of allies and reconciliation. Credibility is earned through learning about the lived experiences of Indigenous people, using the correct terminology, and being open to always learning more.

So many non-Indigenous people have proclaimed their expertise about "Indigenous issues" and solutions, but that is a bit like an adult without children telling a mom how to manage a toddler. Or an urban dweller proclaiming to a third-generation farmer that they know everything about how to drive on dirt roads in the rain. There's no credibility. To be influential, allies need to build their credibility.

Don't rush in to be the ally. The most effective allies listen to Indigenous change-makers, researchers, and leaders. Allies listen to learn more, to do better.

Credibility is about relationship. As Indigenous people build their trust in you, your credibility grows. You cannot be an ally by yourself. Allyship is a team sport, and the leaders on that team are always from the group that stands most to benefit. Allies do not take over the movement; they support from behind it.

Here's the important piece. Relationship is about who you are, not what you do. Ah, there's the link! Any relationship is built on a personal level, and personal relationships are the ones that matter. Your credibility as an ally is also about who you are and how you live your values, not what you do at your nine-to-five job. Indigenous people want to know about you, your family, your skills, your hopes, and your commitment to reconciliation over the long term. Indigenous people want to know where you're from and why are you here.

The first impression you make as an ally is important. The way to do this first impression well is to practice your introduction by covering the all-important question "Where are you from?" First Nations, Inuit, and Métis place high value and importance on land. It's hard to describe the value outside the culture, but it shows up in how Indigenous people answer the question. Generally, Indigenous people answer by noting their traditional land and ancestry in their home community. Indigenous people want to know who you are by your connection to land. When Indigenous people ask non-Indigenous people this question, "Where are you from?" it's about the land. They are asking if you can situate yourself within the tapestry of history of the land by reflecting on your culture of upbringing, how long you have lived on the traditional territories of Indigenous people, and how you have benefitted from that land. Your response is worth practicing so you can share it effectively, as this is your first chance to prove that you are a credible ally as you respect the traditional territories and peoples and recognize that your family is here on the good graces of Indigenous Peoples.

A small hint—if your family has been here for generations, that still does not compare to the thousands of years that Indigenous people have cared for this land. Don't say your family has been here "forever," as you're likely to receive that awkward silence in response as Indigenous people are deciding whether to laugh or call you out, or both. Your family has been here for a sliver of time compared to Indigenous people, even if you can trace your ancestry on this land back to the 1600s.

Indigenous people will next want to know, "Why are you here?" Allies need to bring some good communication skills to convey why you are there to Indigenous people. It's worth taking some time to think through how you will answer that question with humility. Are you here to help? Be careful with how you phrase this, as you do not want to appear to be the saviour. Try to put yourself in the moccasins of Indigenous people and consider how you sound to them. Think through your motivations on why you are an ally. Indigenous people are quite adept at seeing through superficiality, fake answers, and performative actors. Being performative is the antithesis of authenticity and credibility.

Relationship is about being present and part of something bigger. Jonathan Paradis is white from Quebec and has spent years supporting the work led by Inuit in mental health in Nunavut. He lived in Iqaluit for five years. The truth is that many southerners go to live in Iqaluit for the jobs and money, and don't get involved in the community or learn anything about Inuit ways. Jonathan remarked, "What a sad way to live." He chose to connect with Inuit. He built personal relationships with Inuit he worked with, went out on the land to learn from them, and lived his credibility as an ally. Jonathan is known for his authenticity and care.

> Know your place, and be in it for the long run. If you truly care, it can't be a temporary thing. It takes time to build trust; don't waste that precious trust. Because it's never really fully earned.

Jonathan added an important point about allyship. He noted that Québécois culture tends to be more expressive and communicative about emotion and love, more "touchy feely" than Inuit culture. Jonathan easily talks about love in friendships and relationships, and he reflected on his learning about cultural competence that Inuit may not do that in their culture.

> It took me awhile to realize that there was love in the silence we could be in together. I struggled with feeling like I was welcomed, but I think I had been welcomed

Allyship is skill, practice, and art, just like an athlete builds capacity for next-level sports.

by the community before I realized it. It took me some
time to realize the different cultural ways of showing
relationship.

Humility

Allies are humble. Humble is not a bad word. Humility is
a shared value of many Indigenous cultures. Allies who
are humble are much more likely to be respected. Quite
honestly, humility is about being open to the possibility
that you might learn more from Indigenous people than
you give.

Humility also involves a sense that you are not doing
the work for your own good. Sure, building a better
society requires equity, and at some point you will benefit from that better society. But allies are not in it for
the gratification or the personal reward, and certainly
not for the social media. The practice of allyship is
in service of Indigenous people and in the interest of
reconciliation.

Assertiveness is valued in Canadian culture, especially business subculture. You're expected to speak up,
use your voice, take your space, and lead. In job interviews, you might even be asked to provide examples of
when you were assertive. But be aware that assertiveness is not valued the same way, or even at all, in many
Indigenous cultures. Humility is valued more than
assertiveness. In Tlingit culture as well as most First
Nations on the west coast, the longhouse is a place of
ceremony. Longhouse protocol is complex, with two

speakers and an audience, so three actors are involved. Humility is the foundation of it all, so much so that even the first speaker on behalf of a clan might apologize in advance for any mistakes. The responder-speaker role and protocols are also bound by humility. The protocols of how to do ceremony are deeply embedded in the value of humility.

Humility is also about knowing yourself and the privileges that you hold. Don't gloss over those privileges, likely many that Indigenous people do not hold. Please do your internal work to deepen your self-awareness about privilege. It could be in the form of money, it is likely related to your education, and it might be about the colour of your skin. White people hold the highest privilege in Canada. That privilege is unearned, as I certainly did not earn a lack of privilege, right?

Privilege without awareness is dangerous to Indigenous people. If I am not aware that someone I am relating with does not have the same privilege that I do, then I might judge that person unconsciously and think their experience is their own fault... it is because of who they are. Here's an example: When you walk into a hotel, do you ever question whether you will receive excellent service because of the colour of your skin? I often do because I do not have the privilege of white skin, and I wonder if I will have to work to get the attention of the person behind the front desk. If you were to witness the times when I don't get good service, and you expect me to always receive good service as someone with white skin typically does, then you are projecting your experience onto me. But I walk through the world differently, without some of the privileges others hold. Please do not judge me for that lack of privilege. It is not my fault. Nor is it the fault of white people that they hold privilege. But assuming everybody holds privilege is unconscious bias.

When unconscious privilege and unconscious bias are active together, the situation is a mess for the person with less privilege. Fair warning: allies without a sense of their own privilege will encounter distrust from Indigenous people. Unconscious privilege is so annoying that social media is filled with memes about Karen (apologies to learners who are named Karen; it's not about you). Knowledge of your own privilege is a requirement for allies. Because then you can use your privilege in the fight for equity for Indigenous people. Amazing power exists when you know that people will listen to you and you use that to enable Indigenous inclusion. We'll do a deeper dive into privilege in the next chapter.

Commitment

Choosing to practice allyship for Indigenous people is not a year-long checklist. It's a life-long commitment of social justice. It's a way of being.

I asked Julie what allies need to know, and she responded with her driving principle of practice and chosen way of being in the world.

Allyship is about practice, lots of practice. I can't say that this is who I've always been. There was learning that I needed to do to understand the inequities that Indigenous people face. It's about understanding that first. And then practicing looking at every interaction at work, for example, asking yourself, What are my biases here? Asking yourself, Who isn't here? Asking yourself, How can I bring in the voices that are not here? With enough practice, it starts to become instinct. And then you're always asking yourself, How are Indigenous people involved and do they benefit here? It becomes a way of being in the world.

Practicing allyship is a long-term commitment. It doesn't mean that the current job in front of you will be long term. Jonathan Paradis supported Inuit to create a land-based healing centre. He shared that he supported the process by working with bureaucracies to fund it, and then felt it was a good time to move on. The work continued without him, as it should. Indigenous-led work should never be reliant on allies. But be assured that Jonathan will always be working to support Indigenous people and reconciliation.

Commitment to reconciliation is about protecting your value of equity and then acting on that value for your whole life. When you choose to act for equity as a daily practice, then you also protect your credibility as an ally. Allies prove their credibility with each and every new work or project they commit themselves to. If you work with one Indigenous community to bring about a goal they've set, you will start from scratch to build credibility when you start to support another Indigenous community. Don't think of it as repetitive. Think of it as relationship.

Influence

Allies use their influence to support change. Consider this: you have a network of friends who respect your views, and you could build on your relationship with them to share about your passion for reconciliation. Perhaps you can influence them to join you on the journey. Or consider your workplace an opportunity to influence co-workers and peers to learn more about reconciliation. Allies use their influence and networks for reconciliation.

Start conversations with your family and share what you've learned about history and reconciliation. Enter discussions at work by asking, "How would this decision/policy/funding benefit Indigenous people?" Support networks, friends, and work peers in learning more. Changing societies is about changing people's minds. There is a role for you to lead these conversations.

Make space for Indigenous voices. Allies amplify the voices of those who stand to benefit from your support. Is there an event, conference, panel, or book club that you attend that does not include any Indigenous voices? How can you use your influence to ensure that

Indigenous voices are included next time? Allies are best positioned to push change from within, especially in instances when no Indigenous people are involved. Then it is up to you as an ally to build Indigenous inclusion.

When you get involved in a project or with supporting an Indigenous community, take care to follow their lead. Even if you are an expert in your field, you must follow their lead on priorities, sequencing, and decisions. Indigenous communities are also nations with self-determination. Don't bulldoze over their right to make decisions for themselves. Allies support reconciliation and change from behind, never from in front. Just as there would never be a Black Lives Matter event led by a white person, there should never be an ally speaking on behalf of Indigenous people. You can make space for Indigenous voices to take their place on the stage. That is how allies build inclusion, by making space and then modelling respect for Indigenous voices.

There's always time to share your knowledge, as long as you have built the relationship and practice humility. You will know when Indigenous people will ask.

You can tell when someone is an effective ally because they are doing things—they are acting, they are moving. Ally is a verb. While they are still learning about Indigenous people and how to be an effective ally, they are doing things. There is no such thing as an *inactive* ally. The only way to be an ally is to show up and support change as best as you can.

Building awareness in others

Change management is about using time-tested approaches and sequences to change an organization, a company, or a community. In a nutshell, change management is not about changing systems; it is about communicating and influencing and supporting people to change in a system. Change management is about people changing. You will recall that people change by agreeing that there is a problem, that your solution is worthwhile, and that the problem is a priority worth attention now. Next, people decide to be part of the solution, and this is achieved by talking people through it all. There are also technical aspects to training and modelling change, celebrating early wins, and cementing the changes in policy.

Reconciliation is about naming the problem, proposing solutions, and then helping people to together put those solutions into action. Reconciliation is about the hope that we want to do better as a society for Indigenous inclusion and well-being, and that we can make the changes necessary to bring about that change. The first step in making change is to convince others that there is actually a problem. The second step is to propose a solution and get others to join you to make it happen.

The TRC spent significant amounts of time sharing the truths of residential schools to show Canadians the extent of the problem. While Canadians are still learning, we're also at the next step of trying to change things to address the exclusion of Indigenous people and related racism, and the inequities and challenges for Indigenous people to achieve well-being. We are learning and we are doing.

Allies need to be able to describe the problems well enough to build awareness in others. An essential responsibility for allies is to build awareness and agreement with your networks about the issues facing Indigenous people, and then build agreement that these problems can be solved. A problem without a solution is just overwhelming. A solution without a problem will not build support. Allies need to be ready to talk about both, using facts and passion as appropriate to build understanding and agreement.

Practice how to educate and influence others. Practice how to break down the Great Canadian Lie that Indigenous people will not do better and will always need external government oversight. Practice how to break down the status quo argument by comparing the system or funding outcomes experienced by Indigenous people to any other group in Canada. (What if we funded just one province like that? What if a city endured that outcome?) Practice how to lead your network and workplace to a different future that is all about Indigenous inclusion and belonging.

How to close the gap

One of the essential outcomes of reconciliation is to close the gap. This is a phrase to describe how we must as a country close the gaps in Indigenous health outcomes, or just about any statistic in which Indigenous people are not doing as well as non-Indigenous people. Where there's a gap between Indigenous outcomes and non-Indigenous outcomes, we must close those gaps. In fact, closing the gap is one of the measures of reconciliation itself.

There is one aspect of closing the gap that is uniquely suited for the voices of allies, and it's about equity versus equality. I know this sounds like dense policy wonkiness, but please hear me out.

First, the difference between equity and equality. Imagine there's a cliff and a number of people are trying to climb up it, but they are all stuck on this barest sliver of an edge, twelve feet down. Although the people are all balancing precariously on their toes on this little edge on the cliff, the people are all different. There's a six-foot-four man, a five-foot-six woman, and a four-foot-six individual. Picture now there's a person standing on top of the cliff holding a rope yelling, "Just grab the rope!" But the rope only reaches down three feet exactly. It's an "equal" rope for all. The six-foot-four guy easily grabs it and jumps up. The five-foot-six woman can just barely stretch to it and with a lot of effort scrambles up, a bit bloodied but she makes it. The four-foot-six individual can't reach it at all, no matter what they do to try.

Equality says give every person the exact same thing. Same opportunity to live. Same opportunity to not fall off the cliff. In this analogy, equality is actually an argument for the strongest and tallest to thrive while leaving the rest to fall. It sounds just a bit mean, does it not? Too bad for the four-foot-six individual.

In contrast, equity is giving each individual the support they need to get out. It's not about measuring out exactly the same length of rope; it's about giving people what they need to survive and thrive. It's why we want special education supports in schools for children who need it.

Unfortunately, allies will have too much practice on the equality/equity debate. You will find people in your network or at work arguing for equality. Practice your points on how equity is the way in which we ensure every child matters and every child is supported to thrive.

Second, this is an additional and important point on why allies need to perfect how you tell this story about equity and equality. In the cliff analogy, you can imagine that the four-foot-six individual most likely cried in relief when somebody yelled from above, "I'm throwing down a rope!" How could they know that the rope wasn't going to fix the problem? Anything is better than nothing, right? Follow me as I expand on this analogy. There may be Indigenous communities who take the band-aid money offered, as it's better than nothing. A community might take the band-aid money to get a water treatment plant that doesn't come with the piping infrastructure, knowing that new moms and grandmas still will have to walk to get the water, but at least it's clean water. A community may take the band-aid funding for the nursing clinic facility maintenance even though it's not nearly enough to cover the need—at least they can seal in the asbestos in the ceiling, knowing they really need a new clinic built. The truth is that it's incredibly difficult to argue for an equitable solution for one's own community when things are really dire. This is a crucial role for allies: to advocate for equitable solutions and equitable funding that truly fixes the problem facing Indigenous people. This is clearly a role for allies.

Practice your equity advocacy for Indigenous people. We've come through a long era of underfunding, and some communities might decide something is better than nothing yet know it won't truly fix the problem. But you can advocate for real equity and the necessary funding to fix the issues now, so our children aren't left with the problem. No more short ropes. Hell, no more ropes—let's build the elevator!

About apology

I would like to circle back to the point that allyship exists within relationship. The real learning of practicing allyship happens in relationship. So it should not come as a surprise when I say you might make mistakes. We all make mistakes in relationship; we can't really deny it.

I like to set out a lens on the work of allyship that is centred in adult education. Adult education at its heart believes that adults can learn. Seems simple, but it's worth pointing that out. We read, we go to school, we go to university, we go to college, we go to continuing education courses for work, all to learn more. To learn more to do better. Because there was a time when we didn't know. And now we know more. The practice of allyship will push you to continually learn, sometimes from mistakes.

Give yourself some grace that you might make mistakes and you can choose to learn from them.

And then learn how to make a good apology. Good apologies are not glib, they don't gloss over your impact on others, they are not done with speed to try to get past it. Good apologies are done with meaning and authenticity, with recognition of the effect you had on someone, when the time is right for the person who needs to hear it, and with your commitment to learn and do better next time. That is a good apology.

Within many Indigenous cultures, the protocol for making apology or reparation is serious business. Not because it's so difficult, but because doing a good apology can actually solidify a relationship. It strengthens a community.

Sometimes business leaders will say that failure leads to the greatest learning. That is not quite it. When repaired in a good way, failure in a relationship can strengthen that relationship. It is not just about your learning from it; it is about the relationship too. Don't be afraid of making mistakes. Be afraid of not learning from them. A mistake in the action of reconciliation may result in an even stronger relationship with Indigenous people. It's all in relationship, and we all make mistakes in relationships. Learn how to get through it.

Team Reconciliation. We do this together.

— NEXT STEPS —

Sorry, no more checklists. You've done the work, now it's up to you to develop your own next steps.

1. _____

2. _____

3. _____

— RESOURCES —

Indigenous people are much more than just trauma.
Part of the job of an ally is to always look for strength.
It's time to find the joy and laughter in Indigenous people.

Bainbridge, Catherine, and Alfonso Maiorana, dirs. *Rumble: The Indians Who Rocked the World*. Film. Canada: ARTE and Rezolution Pictures, 2017.

Taylor, Drew Hayden. *Motorcycles & Sweetgrass*. Vintage Canada, 2011.

Follow Wab Kinew, the premier of Manitoba, on Instagram @wabber.

Read about Natan Obed, the president of Inuit Tapiriit Kanatami, and his approach (itk.ca).

Watch many of the films of Alanis Obomsawin at the National Film Board of Canada.

6

GETTING COMFORTABLE WITH DISCOMFORT

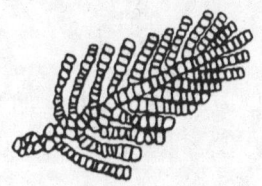

You don't expect things are going to change necessarily in your lifetime, but that doesn't stop you from taking steps to social justice… Children who [see] their parents taking action [are] far more filled with hope.

ARIEL CREIGHTON

HAVE A LARGE and complicated mix of families with my First Nations extended family and my adopted family of British descent. My adopted dad's sister Ariel and her husband, Hugh, provided another home away from home for me while I lived in the Vancouver area as a young adult. At that time, Aunt Ariel worked at the First United Church situated in the Downtown Eastside of Vancouver. The Downtown Eastside has always been a unique neighbourhood with thousands of Indigenous people along with others from across the world. The neighbourhood has a reputation for housing challenges and substance use. I remember it as a melting pot of Indigeneity and a sense of community against all odds.

Aunt Ariel is a mover and shaker in her church community, a trusted voice who somehow always brought people with her on goals of changing the world, also called social justice. She has this way of looking at you with compassion that just melts your resistance. We all know she is authentic. There was power in how she showed compassion to the people our society left behind in the Downtown Eastside that will remain with me all my days.

When I was young, I remember Aunt Ariel talking on the street to an Indigenous individual who was dealing with a number of concurrent issues, including substance use. Ariel is a woman of British descent with privilege, and here she walked right up to this Indigenous individual living on the street and offered a hug, talking to the person like a friend. I had never seen that before. In my short life, I saw so many Canadians walk past and ignore people struggling, Indigenous people on the street. But here she was—a white woman showing compassion. Aunt Ariel always saw strength in humans and in humanity. Make a career out of humanity.

First United Church gave sanctuary to refugees from Guatemala in the early 1990s when that country was in civil war. Indigenous refugees from Guatemala came to Canada to escape certain death, but governments didn't want them here. Hundreds sheltered in churches to escape. Aunt Ariel and the team at First United Church found ways to feed, shelter, and care for Indigenous refugees while authorities dithered about whether the tradition of church sanctuary should be discontinued. I can picture Aunt Ariel on the steps of First United Church, standing to protect the sanctuary. She wouldn't be alone; she would have the quiet riot team of women at First United Church. But we all knew that Ariel would live her values even if there was risk.

Others in the family worried that Aunt Ariel's chosen vocation of compassion might have impacts on her, but I don't believe Ariel viewed it as risk. Aunt Ariel viewed a lack of action in the face of need as the crucial risk to her sense of integrity, as well as the integrity of the community.

I've often wondered about compassion and the lack of it in racism. How do we teach compassion for those around us who are different? Can it be taught? Can it be learned? How is it that Aunt Ariel and others like her don't see difference but instead see community? I believe compassion is a chosen behaviour, often learned through modelling. When you see somebody you trust act on a value, you can see that it's possible. We learn through the modelling of leaders.

Acting on compassion may also have risks for allies. Was it possible that Aunt Ariel might be arrested for protecting the sanctuary for refugees? Possibly, although the risk to her as a privileged white woman was much less than it would have been for the refugees. But it was, and would be still in similar situations, a risk.

Herein is the lesson. Allies who act to bring about change in the world are likely to face resistance, and sometimes that resistance will lead to personal loss to you. I'm not advocating that you go get arrested for your beliefs, but many in this country have done so. I am advocating and pushing you to think about what you're willing to risk for reconciliation. Are you willing to risk your social standing if your network refuses to engage on topics of reconciliation? Next-level allies take personal risks to bring about change, and some might argue that personal risk is the only way to make real change.

But allies do not act and take personal risk just for the story to share on social media. We rarely hear about the risks that next-level allies take, because they don't do it for the story and personal prestige. They take the risk because they are acting on their values and cannot conceive of not acting. The constant refrain from next-level allies is "How could you not?"

There is also a lesson in here about working as a team. Ariel was fully aware of the risks she took. She would have talked over the potential risks with her team, and they would have honestly shared their individual tolerances for risk and then come to consensus on the team's tolerance for risk together. A team working together can accomplish more, but just as importantly, it can risk more.

Are activists and next-level allies required to achieve reconciliation? Yes. Allies are required to make change across systems and to push other non-Indigenous people to do the work as well. In many of the large shifts in Canada that made space for Indigenous people, non-Indigenous activists and allies leaned in to give their weight to the struggle. After World War II, Canada signed on to the Universal Declaration of Human Rights but did not extend those basic human rights to Indigenous people. Because of the international pressure from the UN, Canada eventually extended those rights to Indigenous people. Here's another example. When Inuit were enduring unimaginable tuberculosis rates in the 1950s, the federal government refused to serve them as citizens. During the Cold War, the American military was stationed in the Arctic while building defence systems and radar stations, and was appalled at the plight of Inuit. They went back and told American media. The pressure that resulted from this is what forced the federal government to finally serve Inuit with healthcare for tuberculosis.

The TRC clearly calls non-Indigenous people to action across a multitude of areas. In short, Indigenous people cannot and should not be expected to do the work—almost all of the 94 Calls to Action are intended to be actioned and completed by non-Indigenous Canadians. The systems built up by settler governments need to change, and now is the time for non-Indigenous people to change them to ensure full inclusion for Indigenous people. We need allies.

Start with literacy

Where do you start? With literacy. Literacy leads to allyship, and allyship leads to activism. Allyship without activism is the theory, and theory is a good thing. The belief in Indigenous rights and reconciliation—this is required! A theoretical understanding is required. But reconciliation is more than theory. Allies need to read the books and think through their values, and deepen awareness by talking to others on similar learning journeys. Allies need to do the internal work to commit to caring about Indigenous people.

It's well and good to talk about reconciliation. This is a step in adult education—to talk through your new knowledge. It is important to cement your knowledge about the struggle for Indigenous rights and inclusion by talking about it. Adults also tend to talk about new knowledge with safe people, others who know about the topic or are known to be supportive. Integrating new information is hard enough, so adults tend to find safe places to practice. But if all that occurs is talk between people who agree with each other, what changes? It is practice. All practice is good, but it's still just practice. It is only theoretical.

The next and necessary step is to risk one's own comfort to challenge those who disagree with reconciliation and the rights of Indigenous people. And there is risk. Some Canadians may belittle your choice. Some may berate your values. It is easier to say nothing in the face of racism against an Indigenous individual, but the regret of doing nothing may sting for a much longer time than the discomfort of standing up.

This is the work for next-level allies. Be ready to talk to friends, family, and peers who don't agree with you. Prepare to get out of your comfort zone to challenge others and bring others along with you. When others drop into "status quo-ism," you need to find effective ways to challenge the status quo. When the status quo has never worked for Indigenous people, it needs to change.

Next-level allies question the status quo that historically has excluded Indigenous people. A funny thing about the status quo: it protects itself simply because it can. Allies will find themselves in uncomfortable situations when organizations, systems, and individuals resist in order to maintain the status quo. Perhaps that's how you know you've hit on a key point of reconciliation—the system resists. Don't stop!

Let's be honest: there is probably more than one area of potential discomfort for allies. Indigenous people assume that allies are okay with discomfort, and the absence of discomfort is suspect. If being an ally is easy then you're not taking enough risk.

So, let's get a bit uncomfortable.

Privilege

One discomfort in moving to this next level of allyship is about privilege. There are so many assumptions about the word and most of them are wrong. No, privilege is not a bad word. No, it's not just about money. Privilege exists even if you don't believe in it. Peggy McIntosh, a white professor in the United States, coined a phrase back in the late 1980s, the "invisible knapsack of privilege."

> I have come to see white privilege as an invisible package of unearned assets that I can count on cashing in each day, but about which I was "meant" to remain oblivious. White privilege is like an invisible weightless knapsack of special provisions, assurances, tools, maps, guides, codebooks, passports, visas, clothes, compass, emergency gear, and blank checks.

Part of the essential learning for allies is deepening your understanding of your privilege, because only then can you use it to amplify the voices of Indigenous people. A key process in moving beyond ally to activist is the recognition that privilege has benefitted non-Indigenous Canadians. It has benefitted you, even if you are not aware of it. If your family has been in Canada for more than two generations, your ancestors have likely benefitted from the land taken from Indigenous people, from the natural resources stolen from Indigenous people, from the country's wealth built from the wealth generated out of broken Treaties with Indigenous people. If you are a person of colour, you likely have similar issues with racism and yet you still may hold more privilege than an Indigenous person. No, it's not a competition. Don't let the false flag of competition get in the way here. A socially just society is just for all, not just for a few.

Awareness of your privilege is crucial knowledge that Indigenous people expect you to have. This is how you form credibility as an ally.

Privilege in Canada always gets the benefit of the doubt. As an obviously First Nations–looking woman who cannot pass as white, I know that I don't have that privilege or that benefit of the doubt. For example, a white man caught speeding is much more likely to get the benefit of the doubt from the police officer, while a First Nations man caught speeding is much more likely to not get the benefit of the doubt. That is privilege on one side of the coin, and perhaps racism on the other side.

There are many privileges that, as an Indigenous person in Canada, I do not have: the assumption of others that I am successful; the assurance that almost all of the senior leaders and board members of a hospital look like me; being able to walk down a big city street knowing I am not at risk of racism or being race-carded by police; being treated by doctors and nurses of my own race and culture; knowing healthcare workers will listen to me instead of ignoring me; going shopping alone and being assured that store security is not following me because of my race; knowing my race does not interfere with my ability to get credit, mortgage approvals, housing rentals, and bank accounts; not feeling like I need to have "that conversation" with my kids about how to survive racism.

I do have some privileges, as I have some post-secondary education, a livable income, a network of some amazing leaders in politics and health, and I'm connected to my Tlingit community back home. I know that I hold relatively more privilege than some Indigenous people, and possibly more than some non-Indigenous Canadians. But my list of privileges is still a short list. I did not earn this short list of assurances, and white Canadians did not earn their relatively longer list of assurances. It is unearned. That is the whole point of privilege. But it plays out differently for Indigenous people compared to non-Indigenous people on a daily basis.

Taking space in the reconciliation field does not require you to take off your privilege, like changing clothes, because removing the privilege that you have is simply impossible. Taking space in reconciliation does require you to spend the time to recognize your privilege and be open about it. There's no use in hiding it! If you have some stamps in your passport that Indigenous people don't have, how can you use them to benefit Indigenous people? How can you use those assurances to amplify Indigenous voices? How can you lend your stage to Indigenous reconciliation?

Julie practices allyship at an advanced level.

On a daily basis at work, frankly, you need to put on a lens of Indigenous inclusion. Who's invited to meetings, who is being brought into projects? As a leader, you have to choose who you bring into certain rooms, so how are you able to advance the visibility of Indigenous employees and peers? Are you nominating Indigenous partners, peers, and employees? As a white leader with privilege, it's my responsibility to advance the voices of Indigenous people. But be careful about how you make space for Indigenous voices, because how you do it can sometimes feel paternalistic. So, it has to be done in a way that is empowering and wanted.

Unrecognized privilege taking space in a crowd of Indigenous people is the fastest way to get ignored. Unrecognized privilege looks like the white leaders expecting that they have more expertise and obviously Indigenous people need it. Unrecognized privilege looks like the researcher who parachutes into an Indigenous community with the research question already defined, but that question has no relevance to the community. Unrecognized privilege is making the whole interaction about you and your time, your expertise, your contribution. Allyship needs to include a sense of humility. Practice humility. Please do not add to the stress of Indigenous people by being unaware of your own privilege. This is about how you build your self-awareness so that your privilege is not barging in like a moose into a teepee.

Talk to others about privilege. Watch Indigenous movies and note how Indigenous characters react to instances in which they were doubted, instances in which the character did not have privilege. Watch *Killers of the Flower Moon* and notice how the character Mollie Burkhart, a First Nations woman of privilege in her own community, can't be heard by white people. Watch the 2022 version of the TV series *Dark Winds* and see how the Indigenous character Jim Chee has to fight to be heard by his FBI peers. Watch *Reel Injun*, a documentary about how movie-making didn't even cast Indigenous people in Indigenous roles for decades because of racism. These are all quite realistic portrayals.

The more you learn about privilege, the better you can act as an ally for reconciliation.

Emotion

Emotion is part of the human experience; you can see it as one of the four domains in the medicine wheel, key to many First Nations' knowledge systems. Emotion cannot be shut off; it won't be left behind; it is part of us. And it's what we do with emotion that matters.

Ally discomfort may come in many forms. Some allies get angry, a righteous anger that such inequity exists in this country. Who wouldn't be angry when they learn that Indigenous women and girls are at least twelve times more likely to go missing or be murdered? Who wouldn't be angry to learn that Indigenous kids still are not assured clean drinking water in every community? Wouldn't the average human react with anger to such systemic discrimination? But the absence of anger does make me wonder, why are Canadians not angry?

Anger can give energy. But do not be the angriest one in the room. Be careful that you do not show more energy and emotion than the Indigenous individual who is living through that inequity. Don't grandstand your anger. Choose to work through the anger offstage, and then channel it into being supportive for reconciliation.

Discomfort may also be experienced as sorrow. There is a sadness in realizing, perhaps for the first time, that Canada really does hold Indigenous people back across history but also in the present. There is sorrow in learning more about the challenges faced by Inuit children with mental health challenges without access to supportive services, by Métis parents unable to find healthcare for their children. The more one learns about history and its ongoing impacts on Indigenous people, the more sorrow is expected. Learning about history without sorrow is also suspect. How can one learn about the residential schools and not feel sorrow?

Be aware that an ally cannot have more sorrow than the Indigenous people who lived through it and lost family members who didn't make it. Do not grandstand your sorrow. Choose to use the emotion to build compassion and empathy.

Please work through it and find a way to come to grips with it. Please do not expect an Indigenous person to support you in your sorrow. I do not need to know how much pain you feel to learn about unmarked graves. I do need to know that you are working through it and finding a way to contribute to those children coming home. In the midst of Indigenous pain and loss, you cannot make yourself the centre of the attention. The focus is still on the survivors. But this isn't a new expectation, as you practice this balance of humanity in other places. Likely you've been to a funeral of somebody you cared deeply for outside of your immediate family, and you know how to show grief while respecting the experience of the immediate family. Maybe you even stepped up to support the immediate family with food, water, a chair. That is the essential role of an ally in times of grief and loss.

Some allies feel a weight of guilt for not knowing about all the harms of residential schools, or perhaps a sense of regret for not acting. Guilt is also part of the human experience, but it freezes us in place. Find ways to learn from guilt, to turn it into resolve. Make a list of things that you don't want to do again, a learn-more-to-do-better list, and move through it. There are no tips on moving through guilt, as my tips are for me and not for you. But keep this one thought in mind: Guilt does not always correlate with doing the wrong thing. If it did, the designers of residential schools would have felt guilty. They did not. Guilt is one of the gifts that comes with integrity and compassion.

If there are times when the emotions feel like they're too much, then this is a sign that you need to do some work on balance. I chose the Traditional Medicine beading for this book's cover because it reminds me of a teaching about evergreen trees. This may also be helpful for you. Sometimes we feel emotion that is not ours to carry, and these are the times to get out on the land and walk through evergreen tree forests. On the west coast, walking through the big cedar and fir trees is almost magical. It's because these trees and their needles have a role to play in finding our balance. The needles will gently sieve away the emotion that you are not meant to carry. It is only one way the land brings us balance and healing, and the trees quietly offer this to all of us.

Moral injury

There's an interesting phrase nowadays, "moral injury," that is being used by some to describe the emotional and spiritual impacts on them from learning about another's pain or genocide. I think this is a misuse of the term in the context of residential schools. The phrase "moral injury" started with researchers and supporters of military members coming back from war with ethical and moral internal conflicts with what they were directed to do or what they saw their peers do. Researchers noted: "Potentially morally injurious events, such as perpetrating, failing to prevent, or bearing witness to acts that transgress deeply held moral beliefs and expectations may be deleterious in the long-term, emotionally, psychologically, behaviorally, spiritually, and socially (what we label as *moral injury*)." The treatment for post-traumatic stress disorder did not seem to consistently help soldiers affected by moral injury, so researchers believe moral injury is fundamentally different. Some researchers also think that journalists who cover war and potentially traumatizing events might also risk moral injury.

Some are expanding this concept of moral injury out to a wider net to include allies who see the impacts on minorities and feel a moral or ethical conflict about it. I hear from allies who were significantly impacted by the media reports about the findings of unmarked graves at residential schools, and in those early days some said they did not know how to get over it. Yes, there are a multitude of emotions, and these are best dealt with in the ways that we deal with loss. But they are not in the realm of moral injury.

I'm going to go out on a limb here to suggest we keep the word "moral" and drop the "injury" part of the phrase. Here's why. At some point in the learning journey of reconciliation, one cannot help but realize that governments that should have been trusted to do the right thing obviously did not do the right things for Indigenous people. Church leaders were perpetrating or covering up the abuses in residential schools. I recognize there is a sense of loss. People did things they should not have done. Institutions did wrong and lost their right to be trusted. That is not new in the world; that's an old story told in every society and every country.

But let's be clear: The point of reconciliation is about repairing the harms done to Indigenous people. Let's keep the word "moral" in the discussion, because we need morality to lead in reconciliation, but clearly the injury has been held by residential school survivors and those who did not survive. When you feel a sense of risk to your integrity and values, that's your sign to double down on team building to work as effectively together as you can to make your stand. Use the emotional energy to make a difference. This is not a time to stand down—this is a time for courage. Do it for the survivors.

How can you contribute in meaningful and moral ways as Indigenous communities search unmarked graves? If there is an Indigenous community near you starting a search, ask with respect if there is a way you can volunteer. Take your role to fight against the deniers of unmarked graves. Write to national anti-racism organizations that are not doing anything to combat denialism and demand they do better. Donate to charities supporting the searches. Continue to move, act, and fight for change in every way that you can.

Leverage your networks

So how do you choose to move beyond the discomfort, emotion, loss, and perhaps guilt? Just like any other skill development or sport, you push yourself. Next-level allies do not always know what to do. But they still show up and ask how to help. They are still showing up, asking questions, clarifying their knowledge, and being open to learning more to do better. Next-level allies are the partners and activists we need today for reconciliation.

Where can you make a change? How can you support others to join Team Reconciliation? Start at your workplace and practice being an ally there. Practice making space for Indigenous leaders and peers. Practice facilitating Indigenous inclusion. Review the levels of Indigenous inclusion in employees and leaders, on the board, in procurement, in office art and the names of meeting rooms. Go beyond a good land acknowledgement, make it an excellent Indigenous affirmation, and then push your company to put reconciliation into action. Take risks here to push your organization to write a reconciliation plan. Research other companies and organizations leading reconciliation in the arts, healthcare, governance, and the private sector. Learn more about how to move your workplace into a position of leadership in your sector for reconciliation, and then start building a team that can also champion the

The necessary step is
to risk one's own comfort to
challenge those who disagree
with reconciliation and the
rights of Indigenous people.

cause. Now that you've considered how much Indigenous inclusion your organization is currently providing at your workplace, you might see much more opportunity to apply your ally skills.

How can you use your ally skills to influence your local school board or college for reconciliation? Or your municipal or regional government? Or your local news radio or TV channel? Look around your day-to-day world for Indigenous inclusion or perhaps exclusion. Now that you have deepened your knowledge about institutional racism and Indigenous inclusion, you will likely see much more opportunity to apply your ally skills.

Consider how you might take your advocacy into politics. Does the local municipal, provincial/territorial, or federal riding office of your party have a policy for Indigenous inclusion? Are there Indigenous candidates whom you could support? Are there opportunities for you to use your ally skills to support non-Indigenous candidates in their learning journeys? Next-level allies are needed to influence all levels of politics for reconciliation and real-world Indigenous inclusion.

Respond to resistance

You may know people who don't believe in the goals of reconciliation. These are precisely the people you need to reach. These crucial conversations are difficult and they are necessary. Don't do it alone. These conversations are best done with some advance discussions with your team, Team Reconciliation.

Murray Sinclair was a Commissioner for the TRC. In 2021 in a media interview on the National Day for Truth and Reconciliation, he shared some words of warning.

> The difficulty that Canada faces generally is that there is a group of very vocal, very influential people in Canada who hold significant positions of power who are working hard against reconciliation. People who are holding positions of privilege, who are benefitting from the riches of this country that have been taken away from Indigenous people. The people who have been taught to believe that they are superior to Indigenous people and don't want to think they are not. I said at the end of the TRC report getting to the truth was hard but getting to reconciliation will be harder because I knew that there would be people working very hard, very forcefully, even violently against reconciliation... What are you doing to get rid of that violent vocal force that is holding us all back, holding us all, holding this country back? Because that is what's going to stop reconciliation.

It is a sobering message, but ignoring this message may well sink the whole reconciliation endeavour. Will you have an opportunity to engage with a resister who is forcefully working against reconciliation? Do you see it as a learning opportunity? Adult education would say that "it's all learning"; what if you used this approach even in these really difficult conversations? It's all learning. It might take some of the fear out of the equation. Please try, even with resisters to reconciliation. If you don't try, who will?

I know some readers are looking for clear next steps to be drawn out here. I meant it when I said that the more that you know, the more opportunity you will see to act as an ally. At a certain point on your learning journey, you will start to see more and more opportunities to act. It's a bit like starting a new sport, like football. Football players learn very explicit plays at first, like the running back learning a detailed play that sets out how many steps to run before pivoting to catch the ball. After much practice, players start to get creative and adapt the move. After much practice, teams start to get truly creative together and riff on the plays. Being an ally is like that. At first you follow the coach's drills and directions to develop muscle memory and skill. And then at a certain point, you have enough skill and can truly get creative with your team. Coaches are still there to help you tweak your work on difficult plays and difficult conversations, but it's time for you to wear the Team Reconciliation jersey and stand tall.

I can't tell you what you might do for reconciliation or what your impact will be. It all depends on your commitment to learning about the past and current inequities in this country and your commitment to equity. It depends on your ability to build relationships with Indigenous people based in humility. It depends on your skills in bringing others with you and building the team. If you build up the internal values and how you present, opportunities will become open to you. Probably too many opportunities, to be honest. Do the internal work, and then the reconciliation opportunities will become clear.

Join thousands of Canadians from coast to coast to coast who want to see real change and equity for Indigenous people.

— RESOURCES —

Indigenous Reconciliation Group (IRG). *Toolkit for Doing Reconciliation at Work*. Online course. the-irg.ca/onlinecourses/.

Mathur, Ashok, Jonathan Dewar, and Mike DeGagné, eds. *Cultivating Canada: Reconciliation Through the Lens of Cultural Diversity*. Aboriginal Healing Foundation Research Series, 2011.

7

FINDING HOPE AND VISION

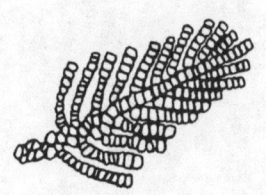

Those who accept the invitation to bear witness [to the stories of residential school survivors] have a responsibility to remember and to take the story forward. It means opening yourself to the truth, allowing yourself to be changed by it... We share a collective responsibility to make things better. To act. Because if we do nothing, nothing will change.

SHELAGH ROGERS

THE JOURNEY of allyship is not quick. My guess is that most allies join the movement out of a sense of necessity, the sense that something must be done. Perhaps they join because of a moral obligation to be part of the solution. At some point on the ally journey, allies need hope, not the easy feeling of it but instead the practice and skill of choosing hope. I think of the old Greek story about Sisyphus, whose punishment from the gods for being wicked was to roll a rock up a hill only to have it roll down again every night. Nobody continues a fight knowing it will all fall apart again tomorrow. We need hope that things will change.

Choosing to be an ally is not easy. It takes a commitment to your learning and to integrating that information. It takes a commitment to spending time building relationships with Indigenous people. Being an ally requires compassion, and with compassion comes the risk of recognizing the pain of others who deserve better. Allies are not immune to the pain of witnessing the inequities Indigenous people experience.

When you choose to open your eyes to the racism that Indigenous people face, or to the inequities across health and education, seeing things improve and envisioning a positive end point is admittedly difficult. In the unique case of Canada, Indigenous people faced and survived generations of legislated racism and segregation, so it is even more challenging to consider a different future.

But we cannot change the past. What is done is done. We need to know our history in order to know where we stand right now. And once we know where we stand now, we have the information needed to determine where we go next.

Allies need to have an accurate grasp of Canada's past, as well as an understanding of the systems of racism that continue to act against Indigenous people. But how do you maintain your energy and commitment? What keeps you committed and acting in the best interests of Indigenous people? Next-level allies are committed for the long term and bring hope. Being an ally means opening yourself to the pain of others, but it also means opening yourself up to the hope of others. And most of all, being an ally requires you to practice your own hope.

Hope has a bit of a messy role in our society. On one hand, movies might talk about hope with a simplistic or even cynical tone. These storylines hold up a hopeful character who might be described as oblivious to reality or endure ridicule. The storylines of movies about hopeful characters usually lead to a dramatic turn in the story when the hopeful person realizes the errors of their ways and "grows up." Our society does not discuss hope with enough depth and understanding, so we make fun of it.

We should talk about hope as a basic human condition, as we really do not want to be without it, right? Hope is what powers change. Hope is what powers a vision that we can do better.

Hope is not a waste, unless we do not act. Hope without action results in nothing. Hope must go hand in hand with action. Hope powered some of the greatest changes that humans have ever done for each other.

Some of the most amazing leaders in the world who fought for the inclusion and respect of marginalized peoples talked about hope as essential in their fight. In the 1950s and 1960s, Dr. Martin Luther King, Jr., was a prominent leader and activist in the civil rights movement in the United States for Black Americans. He said, "We must accept finite disappointment, but never lose infinite hope." Can you imagine the civil rights movement without his influence? Dr. King would have seen the best and the worst of Americans. He saw Black Americans and others gather around his messages of equality and peaceful demonstration. He saw and experienced the legalized racism and segregation of Black people. He saw the white backlash to the movement and riots across Detroit and Newark in 1967 with tens and tens of Black Americans killed, mostly by police. It must have been difficult for Dr. King to maintain his hope and momentum, but he chose hope every day. Not only did he choose hope, but he also chose peaceful action. He was at the front of marches for Black rights. Dr. King chose *ajuinnata*, the Inuktitut word taught to Canadians by Governor General Mary Simon, which means to never give up.

Hope requires resolve.

Mary Simon is Inuk from Kangiqsualujjuaq in Nunavik, Quebec. Before taking on the role of governor general, she used to do more public speaking. She was a special speaker in a course about cultural competence that I was leading, and she encouraged the audience to envision a different future, and then as leaders to take their communities where they've never been before. That is some audacious hope to be able to envision a different way forward.

Hope is more than a feeling. Hope is a choice of the cognitive mind.

Find hope, even on hard days

Why does it matter for reconciliation that hope is a choice backed by resolve? How does hope play into it all? There may be days that are difficult for Indigenous people, and you may be able to hold the hope quietly for many. When an Inuit community loses another family member to police, or when a First Nations community steadfastly reports on the findings of unmarked graves only to be attacked online by residential school denialists, there will be more hard days. Yes, you have compassion and the news affects you. But do not be the outsider who asks for support from Indigenous peers on these days. Do not take the spotlight or demand attention. Instead, provide your own hope that things can get better. Instead of leaning on Indigenous people, choose to be in the football tackle position: stand strong and protect the quarterback. Your role is to block anything else from interfering with Indigenous people's processing of their grief or pain. An ally brings hope even on the darkest days and is ready to share about it when asked.

Michelle Obama said, "You may not always have a comfortable life. And you will not always be able to solve all the world's problems all at once. But don't ever underestimate the impact you can have, because history has shown us that courage can be contagious, and hope can take on a life of its own."

Hope is courageous. Hope brings others along. Hope builds a movement. Hope builds the team. No football game is ever won by an individual. The football moves down the field only because of the team, and so does reconciliation. Reconciliation is advanced by teams, not by individuals. We're trying to overcome generations of pain and change whole systems, and this requires people working together. The good news is that your hope can galvanize others to join, and the team continues to build. The even better news is that working together in teams—be it your team at work or your book club or family or close network—is easier than working alone.

Courageous hope with action builds the teams that power reconciliation. Choose Team Reconciliation. We want all the help we can get.

In my youth, I used to hike on the west coast, the Cascade Range and the Coast Range near Vancouver. An experienced hiker taught me a lesson that had wide-ranging application. When you're on the trail, regularly turn around and look back to remember where you came from, and then look forward and focus on the destination. It sounds so simple, right? Back in the days before GPS and detailed coloured maps on cellphones, we relied on paper maps and compasses to know where we were. And you always looked back so on the return trip, it looks familiar—you know where you came from.

When you start out on a hike or a journey, it seems so easy. I'm here and I'm going there. Sometimes you can even see "there," the mountain peak in the distance. But then the trail gets difficult. Those pesky valleys between you and your destination, the tall trees that block the sun, the overbearing heat or the sudden storm. They drain you. But the most draining thing of all is realizing you might be lost. Not knowing where you are on the trail. "Am I halfway there or just a few minutes from my destination? Am I completely off the trail?" This is the stuff that bursts hope like a punctured balloon. It takes serious discipline to not panic, to work through the problem of being lost. The lesson here is that we need to know where we've been in order to know where we're going, as this is a core part of hope. Don't get lost in the valleys.

A vision for reconciliation

It's worth a moment to put this point in time of reconciliation in context. For centuries, Canadians lived in a bubble of isolation, away from the successes and challenges of Indigenous people. It was almost as if we had a Berlin Wall of our own right through this country, keeping settlers and Indigenous people apart. It started with racism and the Indian Act, reserves and segregation. Settler towns sprung up and pushed Indigenous people away instead of maintaining the Treaties to live together. Hockey leagues were generally segregated so settlers

Courageous hope builds up the movement and Team Reconciliation.

didn't play Indigenous teams. Schools were segregated, with First Nations in on-reserve schools. If I had a dollar for every Canadian who I heard say that there was a First Nations reserve right across the highway from their town but they never interacted with them, I'd be rich. Or vice versa for every First Nations person who said they never crossed that highway into town. In the space of a generation, this wall has crumbled, but not completely.

All to say, this country was built with a Berlin Wall of isolation. The governments liked it that way and even wrote laws to maintain it. The federal government built quite the curtain between us all by facilitating the Great Canadian Lie: "Indigenous people lack capacity and need the government, and that's just the way it is. See, that's why we had to do residential schools, and why we had to put in those racist laws to treat them differently. That's why they need to be separate. Don't worry," they said, "we're supporting them." The Great Canadian Lie facilitated a lack of compassion by Canadians in the face of Indigenous inequities.

So when the stories of residential schools started to come out in the 1990s and 2000s, settler Canadians gave the side-eye and moved on. These stories did not jibe with what they were told about history. Didn't the government create these schools out of benevolence? Indigenous people must have wanted them or needed them. The needle on reconciliation didn't budge.

When the TRC released its Final Report, the beginnings of doubt started to land in the public's mind. "Did the government do all that? That sounds bad. But all those stories of abuse? That's just too much, it can't be... How are the Vancouver Canucks doing?"

But the news of unmarked graves tore down that Great Canadian Lie and replaced it with sorrow and compassion. With compassion comes an internal resolve to do something, to be part of the solution.

But now what? We need vision. We need to picture what it could be like when we achieve reconciliation. Hope needs a map and end point.

Consider what would need to change in systems to do real reconciliation.

What if federal and provincial/territorial politics, even municipal politics, did reconciliation? And political parties and debates and platforms relied on Indigenous voices and knowledges, rather than ignored them? What would have to change to bring that about? Maybe we'd see better decisions made in political realms.

What if provincial and territorial ministries of health, on behalf of the healthcare field, apologized for the historical and current-day racism against Indigenous people? And started to care about what happens in Indigenous community healthcare rather than just ignoring it? What if healthcare systems partnered with Indigenous communities, learned from their holistic models of care, and deeply valued Indigenous healthcare leadership? What would have to change? Maybe we would witness the resurgence of humanity in healthcare.

What if schools across all provinces and territories fulfilled their promise made in 2015 to fully include Indigenous knowledges and peoples, instead of giving lip service and one-off special speakers to the topic? What would have to change to ensure that every teacher was fully culturally competent and able to teach about culture and model culturally safe classrooms? What if every school administrator was held accountable to eradicate racism and learn the Indigenous language of the land on which that school is located? What if provincial and territorial school curriculums started first with Indigenous knowledges of this land and then added on mainstream knowledges next, flipping the paradigm, so to speak? What would have to change? Maybe we would live to see the end of racism as children are taught about culture, cultural competence, and valuing Indigenous people and knowledges as essential to Canada.

Those would be wholesale changes in systems. But the quiet fact in any change is that it starts with people. People see the problem and decide to do something about the problem. People change. People learn more to do better, and then systems reflect the people. So we are the change.

Imagine the near future, let's say twenty years in the future. If we were to set a future further out than that, we might let ourselves off the hook and wait for somebody else to do the work. But twenty years, that is within our responsibility and our influence.

Imagine a First Nations community in northern Ontario. A young couple is about to welcome their first child. Let's just set the stage that this couple has all the health supports that they need. They prepare for the birth by talking to the nurses and doctors who are available twenty-four hours a day in that small community, as well as Elders and aunties and uncles. Then comes the day when this small human travels over to our side, and the parents are surrounded by aunties and uncles and grandparents and Elders, born on the land of their ancestors. Not born far away in a sterile hospital alone. Because we believe in access to healthcare close to home, and we made it happen for Indigenous communities.

Imagine that young family is supported by their community, by aunties and uncles and sisters and brothers who come alongside and surround that child in the protocols that built strong humans in strong community for generations. Imagine that young human starts to speak in the traditional language first, the language of the land. And learns the community ceremonies, art, song, and dance, which are the baskets of knowledge. Because we know that Indigenous languages and knowledge systems hold unique and invaluable space in a world challenged by climate change, and we protected and supported them to thrive.

Imagine that young human is supported with early childhood programs on the land, learning from peers and aunties and uncles. Imagine that young human then going to school in community, with facilities just like we would expect in any urban school. Because Canada put its money where its mouth is, every child matters. But this school is even better than mainstream schools, because teachers and Elders share space together to see things from all sides. Because we believe in education, so we funded it to succeed in every Indigenous community.

And imagine that as the child grows into a youth, they never experience racism. Because we believe in each other, and we mandated the education for accurate Canadian history, cultural competence, and compassion in every school in the country.

As that young human comes of age in ceremony, they can do whatever they want to do to give back. This person could be a doctor, a nurse, a health technician. This person could be a police officer, a police chief, or a judge. This person could design the greatest buildings of a generation. They could be an artist, a poet, a prime minister. Because that human is proud of who they are, proud to be Indigenous.

Isn't this what we want for all of our children? The freedom to explore the world and self without fear. The safety to learn and grow. The opportunities to give back. If every child matters, then we have our work cut out for us. Whole systems have to change, and it is urgent. This is not work to delay or underfund. Every delay in reconciliation is a statement that every child does not matter today. If we say every child matters, this generation of children must see change.

Reconciliation is urgent. Practice hope; build up the team; show up for Indigenous neighbours, friends, and networks. Practice infinite hope and do the work in your sphere of influence. Build Team Reconciliation. Keep your vision on the goal of reconciliation. We can do this.

For all our children.

ACKNOWLEDGEMENTS

The work that I do is on the shoulders of so many who have gone before me, and on the land that supports me. I am a proud member of the Taku River Tlingit First Nation and thank all my ancestors who survived so I can stand here today. I am currently a grateful guest on the territory of the Algonquin Nation and thank them for the ability to write this book while sitting at a campfire on the river. This book is pre-smudged for your reading pleasure.

I could not have written this book without the powerful teaching and mentoring of Elders. I am in debt to Elder Woody Morrison and Elder Mason Durie, amazing individuals who both saw the world as it is—overflowing with grace and pain and potential—and did their best to try to improve it. I do my best to uphold your belief in me.

To Sandra Scarth, who supported my early career path as a challenger to the system, who modelled ethical leadership, who lived reconciliation even before the TRC. I can't imagine what my career path would have been without your leadership. Thank you, Nicole Fournier-Sylvester, as obviously this book was because of you—you made the connections and pushed me in those early days of doubt. Thank you to Page Two and Rony and Kendra for your kindness and professionalism. Thank you to my adopted family who have always pushed me to further my education and my voice, especially my sister Elda.

To the Official Book Emergency Response Group of Lucie, Frankie, Luc, Julie, Andrew, and Anna, who reviewed key passages and points to offer your thoughtful perspectives, I couldn't have done it without you. Your reasoned input and collaboration were crucial.

To Tanya Talaga, who believed in me and shared so much with me about being a real author, ekosani and miigwech for your courage and leadership.

To Destine Lord, who taught me so much about facilitation and teaching in a good way. You know I could not have done it without you. I know we have more to do together, and I'm honoured to stand with you in the fight. Gunul'cheesh, my friend.

To Kari Nisbet, who keeps me on the high ground as best as you can, who pushes me to do better, who is the glass half-full. Maarsii doesn't even come close to describe my gratitude.

Thank you to my family for putting up with my long periods of absence during this writing process. To my wife, Michele, who empowered me to leave the Government of Canada, to speak openly about Canada's future, to write about things that I care about, and to have hope. I couldn't have done it without you.

And to my daughter, Alex, you are my Northern Star. Stand proud, beautiful.

ODAWA, AUGUST 2024

NOTES

Putting Allyship into Action

p. 5   *"redress the legacy of residential schools":* Truth and Reconciliation Commission of Canada, *Truth and Reconciliation Commission of Canada: Calls to Action*, 2015, the-irg.ca/docs/truth-and-reconciliation-commissions-calls-to-action/.

Chapter 1: Reconciliation Starts with You

p. 8   *"Where do you begin":* Lee Maracle, *Ravensong: A Novel* (Vancouver: Press Gang Publishers, 1993).

p. 12 *By 2023, only thirteen Calls to Action:* Eva Jewell and Ian Mosby, *Calls to Action Accountability: A 2023 Status Update on Reconciliation* (Toronto: Yellowhead Institute, 2023), yellowheadinstitute.org/wp-content/uploads/2023/12/YI-TRC-C2A-2023-Special-Report-compressed.pdf.

p. 13 *the death toll from tuberculosis in some schools:* P.H. Bryce, *The Story of a National Crime: Being an Appeal for Justice to the Indians of Canada* (Ottawa: James Hope & Sons, 1922), caid.ca/AppJusIndCan1922.pdf.

p. 18 *South Africa chose to do reconciliation in the courtroom:* Antjie Krog, *Country of My Skull: Guilt, Sorrow, and the Limits of Forgiveness in the New South Africa* (New York: Crown, 2000).

p. 19 *In the end, Canada chose a relational and healing approach:* Rosemary L. Nagy, "The Scope and Bounds of Transitional Justice and the Canadian Truth and Reconciliation Commission," *International Journal of Transitional Justice* 7, no. 1 (2013): 52–73, doi.org/10.1093/ijtj/ijs034.

p. 20 *Germany went through a process of reconciliation:* Lothar Wigger and Marie Dirnberger, eds., *Remembrance—Responsibility—Reconciliation: Challenges for Education in Germany and Japan* (Germany: J.B. Metzler, 2022).

p. 20 *Almost every German family:* Susan Neiman, *Learning from the Germans: Race and the Memory of Evil* (New York: Farrar, Straus and Giroux, 2019).

p. 20 *the German government made a significant policy decision:* Monica Vitale and Rebecca Clothey, "Holocaust Education in Germany: Ensuring Relevance and Meaning in an Increasingly Diverse Community," FIRE: *Forum for International Research in Education* 5, no. 1 (2019): 44–62.

Chapter 2: Unpacking the Great Canadian Lie

p. 32 *"The circumstances of Indian existence":* J.S. Milloy, *"Suffer the Little Children": The Aboriginal Residential School System, 1830–1992*, submitted to the Royal Commission on Aboriginal Peoples, 1996, data2.archives.ca/rcap/pdf/rcap-126.pdf.

p. 37 *On Turtle Island, in the twelfth century:* Kayanesenh Paul Williams, *Kayanerenkó:wa: The Great Law of Peace* (Winnipeg: University of Manitoba Press, 2018).

p. 40 *when a smallpox epidemic hit in 1862–63:* Kiran Van Rijn, "'Lo! The Poor Indian!': Colonial Responses to the 1862–63 Smallpox Epidemic in British Columbia and Vancouver Island," *Canadian Bulletin of Medical History* 23, no. 2 (2006): 541–61, doi.org/10.3138/cbmh.23.2.541.

p. 42 *extermination, slavery, insulation, or amalgamation:* John F. Leslie, "Commissions of Inquiry into Indian Affairs in the Canadas, 1828–1858," Indian Affairs and Northern Development Canada, 1985, publications.gc.ca/collections/collection_2017/aanc-inac/R5-273-1985-eng.pdf.

p. 43 *He advocated that Manitoulin Island be that place:* Theodore Binnema and Kevin Hutchings, "The Emigrant and the Noble Savage: Sir Francis Bond Head's Romantic Approach to Aboriginal Policy in Upper Canada, 1836–1838," *Journal of Canadian Studies* 39, no. 1 (2004): 115–38, doi.org/10.3138/jcs.39.1.115.

p. 44 *Indigenous communities got so effective at it:* Canadian House of Commons, Sessional Papers, vol. 25.14 (1891), 193; Canadian House of Commons, Sessional Papers, 1889, no. 10.

p. 45 *On Tuesday, March 21, 1876:* House of Commons Debates, 3rd Parliament, 3rd session, vol. 1, parl.canadiana.ca/view/oop.debates_HOC0303_03/790.

p. 46 *"Indians were not in the same position":* House of Commons Debates, 3rd Parliament, 3rd session.

p. 47 *"get rid of the Indian problem":* National Archives of Canada, Record Group 10, volume 6810, file 470-2-3, volume 7, pp. 55 (L-3) and 63 (N-3).

p. 48 *The original Indian Act would be shockingly illegal:* A revised version of the original Indian Act is still a law of Canada. Yes, it is unconstitutional as it sets out segregated systems of education, healthcare, and policing for First Nations from other Canadians. But it is so entrenched in how Canada does business that it seems impossible to eliminate it. Maybe this is an end goal of reconciliation?

p. 52 *"I have reason to believe that the agents":* House of Commons Debates, 4th Parliament, 4th Session, vol. 1, parl.canadiana.ca/view/oop.debates_HOC0404_04/2.

p. 57   *However, the Universal Declaration of Human Rights and the weight:* Jennifer Tunnicliffe, *Resisting Rights: Canada and the International Bill of Rights, 1947–76* (Vancouver: UBC Press, 2019).

Chapter 3: Challenging Interpersonal Racism

p. 66   *"No one is born hating another person":* Nelson Mandela, *Long Walk to Freedom: The Autobiography of Nelson Mandela* (Boston: Little, Brown, 1994).

p. 69   *From reports in the city of Ottawa, British Columbia, Alberta, and more: In Plain Sight: Addressing Indigenous-Specific Racism and Discrimination in B.C. Health Care,* Addressing Racism Review Summary Report, November 2020, engage.gov.bc.ca/app/uploads/sites/613/2020/11/In-Plain-Sight-Summary-Report.pdf; Wabano Centre for Aboriginal Health in Partnership with the Ottawa Aboriginal Coalition, *Share Your Story: Indigenous-Specific Racism in Health Care Across the Champlain Region: Full Report,* wabano.com/wp-content/uploads/2022/05/ShareYourStory-FullReport-EN.pdf.

p. 72   *"access-to-information request revealed":* Greg Mercer, Willow Fiddler, and Marieke Walsh, "N.B. Police Shooting of an Indigenous Woman Sparks Outrage Across Canada," *Globe and Mail,* June 5, 2020, theglobeandmail.com/canada/article-nb-police-shooting-of-indigenous-woman-sparks-outrage-across-canada/.

Chapter 4: Challenging Institutional Racism

p. 86   *"Numerous studies have confirmed":* Honourable John McKay, Chair, *Systemic Racism in Policing in Canada: Report of the Standing Committee on Public Safety and National Security,* June 2021, 43rd parliament, 2nd session (Speaker of the House of Commons, 2021), ourcommons.ca/Content/Committee/432/SECU/Reports/RP11434998/securp06/securp06-e.pdf.

p. 91   *A household in Thunder Bay, Ontario, might pay:*
Andrew Reeves, "Water's True Cost," *Great Lakes Now*,
May 18, 2022, greatlakesnow.org/2022/05/canada
-aging-infrastructure-rising-costs/.

p. 91   *a household in Vancouver might pay:* Derrick Penner,
"What You Pay for Drinking Water in Metro Vancouver
Varies Dramatically Depending on Where You Live,"
Vancouver Sun, April 9, 2024, vancouversun.com/news/
local-news/what-you-pay-for-drinking-water-varies
-dramatically-depending-on-where-you-live.

p. 93   *"found that the total historical spending since 2011–2012":*
Clean Water for First Nations: Is the Government
Spending Enough? (Ottawa: Office of the Parliamentary
Budget Officer, 2021), 5, pbo-dpb.ca/en/publications/RP
-2122-021-M--clean-water-first-nations-is-government
-spending-enough--eau-potable-premieres-nations
-gouvernement-depense-t-il-assez.

p. 93   *"the historical spending since 2016–2017":* Clean Water for
First Nations, 12.

p. 94   *The federal government is paying out a settlement:* Oscar
Baker III, "First Nations Drinking Water Settlement
Open for Claims from Communities, Individuals," CBC
News, March 11, 2022, cbc.ca/news/indigenous/first
-nations-water-drinking-settlement-1.6382206.

p. 95   *In 2024, the tab passed $40 billion:* Darren Major and
Olivia Stefanovich, "Judge Approves Historic $23B
First Nations Child Welfare Compensation Agreement,"
CBC News, October 24, 2023, cbc.ca/news/politics/
judge-approves-23-billion-first-nations-child-welfare
-agreement-1.7006351.

Chapter 5: Lending Your Voice, Influence, and Privilege

p. 102 *"Empathy is the most powerful emotional force":* Anita
Nowak, *Purposeful Empathy: Tapping Our Hidden*
Superpower for Personal, Organizational, and Social
Change (Minneapolis: Broadleaf Books, 2023).

p. 103 *a person "that is associated with another"*: "Ally," *Merriam-Webster.com Dictionary*, merriam-webster.com/dictionary/ally, accessed September 27, 2024.

p. 104 *"An ally is not only about what you do"*: Destine Lord, in conversation with the author, June 2024.

p. 105 *"When you have privilege"*: Dr. Julie Cafley, in conversation with the author, July 2024.

p. 106 *"education, humility, and humanity"*: Angie Seth, in conversation with the author, June 2024.

p. 107 *"Make a career of humanity"*: Martin Luther King, Jr., "Address at the Youth March for Integrated Schools on 18 April 1959," The Martin Luther King, Jr. Research and Education Institute, Stanford University, kinginstitute.stanford.edu/king-papers/documents/address-youth-march-integrated-schools-18-april-1959.

p. 111 *"It took me awhile to realize"*: Jonathan Paradis, in conversation with the author, June 2024.

p. 116 *"Allyship is about practice"*: Cafley, July 2024.

Chapter 6: Getting Comfortable with Discomfort

p. 128 *"You don't expect things are going to change"*: "Making Room for Women Project: Interview with Ariel Creighton," interview by Melanie Ihmels, February 28, 2014, BC Conference, The United Church of Canada, The Bob Stewart Archives, Vancouver, pacificmountain.ca/wordpress2021/wp-content/uploads/Ariel-Creighton-interview-transcript-AC.pdf.

p. 136 *"I have come to see white privilege"*: Peggy McIntosh, "White Privilege: Unpacking the Invisible Knapsack" in *Peace and Freedom Magazine*, 1989, 10–12, a publication of the Women's International League for Peace and Freedom, Philadelphia, PA.

p. 139 *"On a daily basis at work"*: Cafley, July 2024.

p. 144 *"Potentially morally injurious events"*: Brett T. Litz, Nathan Stein, Eileen Delaney, Leslie Lebowitz, William

P. Nash, Caroline Silva, and Shira Maguen, "Moral Injury and Moral Repair in War Veterans: A Preliminary Model and Intervention Strategy," *Clinical Psychology Review* 29, no. 8 (2009): 695–706, doi.org/10.1016/j.cpr.2009.07.003.

p. 149 *"The difficulty that Canada faces generally"*: "'It's Like Renewing Our Vow': Murray Sinclair Says It Will Take a While to Figure Out September 30 but We Shouldn't Give Up," APTN News, September 30, 2021, aptnnews.ca/featured/its-like-renewing-our-vow-murray-sinclair-says-it-will-take-a-while-to-figure-out-sept-30-but-we-shouldnt-give-up/.

Chapter 7: Finding Hope and Vision

p. 154 *"Those who accept the invitation"*: Shelagh Rogers, "Reflections on Being an Honorary Witness for the TRC," CBC News, March 29, 2014, cbc.ca/news/indigenous/reflections-on-being-an-honorary-witness-for-the-trc-1.2587064.

p. 157 *"We must accept finite disappointment"*: Martin Luther King, Jr., Washington, D.C., address in February 1968, *In My Own Words*, compiled by Coretta Scott King (Hodder & Stoughton, 2002).

p. 159 *"You may not always have a comfortable life"*: Michelle Obama, "Remarks by the First Lady During Keynote Address at Young African Leaders Forum," The White House, Office of the First Lady, June 22, 2011, obamawhitehouse.archives.gov/the-press-office/2011/06/22/remarks-first-lady-during-keynote-address-young-african-women-leaders-fo.

ABOUT THE AUTHOR

ROSE LEMAY is a speaker, trainer, and coach on reconciliation—and an unrelenting champion for the inclusion and well-being of Indigenous peoples. As a facilitator and trainer in cultural competence and antiracism, she has supported thousands of Canadians from coast to coast to deepen their understanding and capacity for reconciliation. As a keynote speaker, she can take people through difficult topics of racism and reconciliation to find common ground and hope for the future. LeMay has over twenty years of experience in policy and program development in health and mental health systems in government and the non-profit sector. She is an alumnus of the Governor General's Canadian Leadership Conference, a Certified First Nations Health Manager, certified in Prosci Change Management, and a 2021 Global Pluralism finalist. LeMay is from Taku River Tlingit First Nation in northern British Columbia.

Deepen Your Skills as an Ally

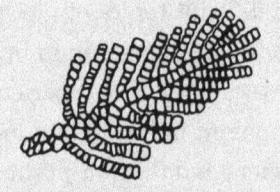

Thanks for finishing my book, wow! Could you do me a favour and write a review at your favourite online retailer? Gunul'cheesh!

Need to advance reconciliation at your workplace or book club? How about buying this book in bulk? Bulk orders of one hundred or more copies receive a discount. Please reach out to **info@the-irg.ca** for more information.

Look me up at **the-irg.ca** for information on my online courses to support reconciliation, my keynote speaking, and my coaching for organizations and leaders doing reconciliation. I'm on LinkedIn, and who knows, I might even expand my old Gen-X horizons to Instagram.

www.ingramcontent.com/pod-product-compliance
Lightning Source LLC
LaVergne TN
LVHW030242250326
834688LV00047B/1761